NOV - - 2004

W9-BCI-728

24
INSECTS
AND OTHER INVERTEBRATES
INSECTS 3

True Bugs

ROD PRESTON-MAFHAM

GROLIER

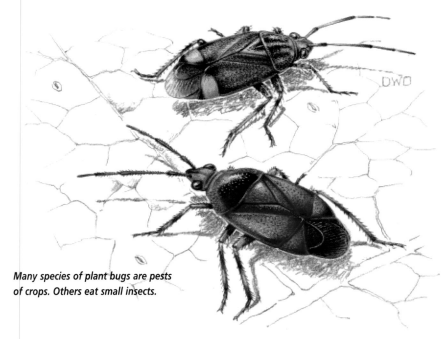

Many species of plant bugs are pests of crops. Others eat small insects.

Published 2004 by Grolier, an imprint of
Scholastic Library Publishing
Danbury, CT 06816

This edition published exclusively for the school
and library market

The Brown Reference Group plc.
(incorporating Andromeda Oxford Limited)
8 Chapel Place
Rivington Street
London
EC2A 3DQ

Library of Congress Cataloging-in-Publication Data

Insects and other invertebrates.
    p. cm. -- (World of animals ; 21-30)
    Contents: v. 21. Simple and wormlike animals -- v. 22. Insects 1: millipedes and unusual insects -- v. 23. Insects 2: crickets, grasshoppers, and flies -- v. 24. Insects 3: true bugs -- v. 25. Insects 4: beetles -- v. 26. Insects 5: butterflies and moths -- v. 27. Insects 6: wasps, bees, and ants -- v. 28. Crustaceans -- v. 29. Arachnids -- v. 30. Mollusks and echinoderms.
    ISBN 0-7172-5894-7 (set) -- ISBN 0-7172-5895-5 (v. 21) -- ISBN 0-7172-5896-3 (v. 22) -- ISBN 0-7172-5897-1 (v. 23) -- ISBN 0-7172-5898-X (v. 24) -- ISBN 0-7172-5899-8 (v. 25) -- ISBN 0-7172-5900-5 (v. 26) -- ISBN 0-7172-5901-3 (v. 27) -- ISBN 0-7172-5902-1 (v. 28) -- ISBN 0-7172-5903-X (v. 29) -- ISBN 0-7172-5904-8 (v. 30)
    1. Insects--Juvenile literature. 2. Invertebrates--Juvenile literature. [1. Insects. 2. Invertebrates.] I. Grolier (Firm) II. World of animals (Danbury, Conn.) ; v. 21-30.

QL467.2.15875 2004
595.7--dc22

2003063100

Project Director: Graham Bateman
Editors: Virginia Carter, Angela Davies
Art Editor and Designer: Steve McCurdy
Editorial Assistants: Marian Dreier, Rita
        Demetriou
Picture Manager: Claire Turner
Picture Researcher: Vickie Walters
Production: Clive Sparling

Origination: Unifoto International, South Africa

Printed in China

Set ISBN 0-7172-5894-7

About This Volume

This volume has been given the title *True Bugs* because of the confusing way in which the word "bug" is used in this day and age. A bug can be a disease, such as a cold, or it can be a problem in a piece of computer software. It is also used to describe almost any small arthropod, including woodlice, spiders, and any kind of insect. The word "bug," however, was originally given to those insects in the order Hemiptera, the true bugs of this volume.

The Hemiptera is subdivided into three suborders, the Auchenorrhyncha, the Sternorrhyncha (both originally combined in a single suborder, Homoptera), and the Heteroptera. Members of the Auchenorrhyncha and the Sternorrhyncha are all plant feeders, using their sucking mouthparts to obtain sap from their specific food plants. Some quite large insects, notably the cicadas and some lanternflies, are included within this group.

The Heteroptera also contains many plant feeders. They likewise have sucking mouthparts that pierce the plant's stem in order to feed. However, many of them, such as the deadly assassin bugs, also use their sucking mouthparts to feed on the body fluids of other arthropods. In the case of a few species this can include the blood of birds and mammals, and even humans.

Contents

The spikes on the backs of thorn bugs mimic the thorns of their favorite food plants, providing protection from predators.

The shield bug's bright colors indicate that it is foul tasting.

Scentless plant bugs feed mainly on the fruits, seeds, and young shoots of plants.

How to Use This Set

World of Animals: Insects and Other Invertebrates is a 10-volume set that describes in detail creatures from all corners of the globe. Each volume brings together those groups that share similar characteristics or have similar lifestyles. This set contains a huge diversity of animal types. To help you find the volumes containing animals that interest you, look at pages 6 to 7 (Find the Animal). A brief introduction to each volume is also given on page 2 (About This Volume).

Article Styles

Each volume contains two types of article. The first kind introduces major groups (such as the animal kingdom, mollusks, insects, or flies). It presents a general overview of the subject. The second type of article makes up most of each volume. It concentrates on describing in detail important groups often with familiar names, such as tarantulas, octopuses, or seed bugs. Each such article starts with a fact-filled data panel to help you gather information at a glance. Used together, the two styles of article enable you to become familiar with animals in the context of their evolutionary history and biological relationships.

A number of other features help you navigate through the volumes and present you with helpful

Data panel presents basic statistics of each animal group

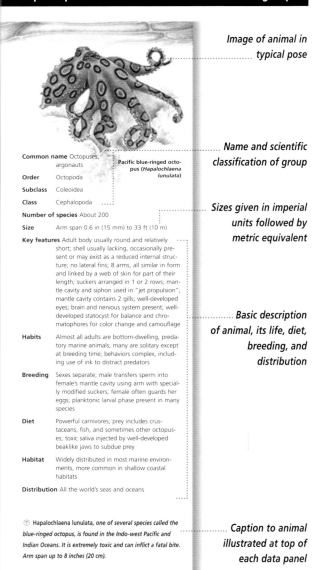

Image of animal in typical pose

Common name Octopuses, argonauts

Pacific blue-ringed octopus (*Hapalochlaena lunulata*)

Name and scientific classification of group

Order Octopoda

Subclass Coleoidea

Class Cephalopoda

Number of species About 200

Size Arm span 0.6 in (15 mm) to 33 ft (10 m)

Sizes given in imperial units followed by metric equivalent

Key features Adult body usually round and relatively short; shell usually lacking, occasionally present or may exist as a reduced internal structure; no lateral fins; 8 arms, all similar in form and linked by a web of skin for part of their length; suckers arranged in 1 or 2 rows; mantle cavity and siphon used in "jet propulsion"; mantle cavity contains 2 gills; well-developed eyes; brain and nervous system present; well-developed statocyst for balance and chromatophores for color change and camouflage

Habits Almost all adults are bottom-dwelling, predatory marine animals; many are solitary except at breeding time; behaviors complex, including use of ink to distract predators

Breeding Sexes separate; male transfers sperm into female's mantle cavity using arm with specially modified suckers; female often guards her eggs; planktonic larval phase present in many species

Basic description of animal, its life, diet, breeding, and distribution

Diet Powerful carnivores; prey includes crustaceans, fish, and sometimes other octopuses; toxic saliva injected by well-developed beaklike jaws to subdue prey

Habitat Widely distributed in most marine environments, more common in shallow coastal habitats

Distribution All the world's seas and oceans

⊕ *Hapalochlaena lunulata, one of several species called the blue-ringed octopus, is found in the Indo-west Pacific and Indian Oceans. It is extremely toxic and can inflict a fatal bite. Arm span up to 8 inches (20 cm).*

Caption to animal illustrated at top of each data panel

Article describes important groups with familiar names

Scientific name of group

Common name of group

Captions to photographs provide additional information about each animal's lifestyle

TRUE BUGS

Lygaeidae

Seed Bugs

Seed bugs is an appropriate common name for the Lygaeidae, since the majority feed on seeds of a range of plant species, including trees. They are also called ground bugs because they feed on seeds that have fallen from the plant onto the ground.

Trapezonotus arenarius

Lygaeus kalmii

Common name Seed bugs (ground bugs)

Family Lygaeidae

Suborder Heteroptera

Order Hemiptera

Number of species About 3,000 (295 U.S.)

Size from about 0.09 in (2.2 mm) to 0.8 in (20 mm)

Key features Rather tough-bodied bugs, mostly oval in shape, some longer and thinner species; body usually appears flat topped; ocelli present, fully and partially winged as well as wingless forms and species; front femurs enlarged in many species; most are combinations of black and brown, a few are brightly colored

Habits Found either on the plant that produces seeds on which they feed or running around on the ground beneath

Breeding Sound production is involved in courtship in many seed bugs; eggs usually laid on or into food plants

Diet The vast majority are seed feeders, others specialize in insect eggs and larvae; a few are blood suckers

Habitat Forests, grasslands, meadows, gardens, marshes, seashore, and deserts

Distribution Worldwide

SEED BUGS ARE AMONG the drabbest-colored bugs, with most being shades of brown to black. There are, however, notable exceptions such as the warningly colored, distasteful large milkweed bugs of the genus *Oncopeltus*, which have black-and-orange patterning.

While most seed bugs live away from the coast, a few species are found on the seashore, including salt marshes. *Henestaris* species from Europe and Asia live in such habitats, as well as inland alongside salt pans. *Henestaris halophilus* is widespread in the region and is also found in a few salt marshes, *Atriplex portulacoides* As the tide comes in, the nymphs remain submerged on the food plant without coming to harm.

Saliva Injection

Seed-feeding Lygaeidae inject saliva into the seed to digest it before sucking up the liquid that results. Those that do not feed on seeds but on the plants themselves puncture single or groups of plant cells and suck the sap out of them. With around 3,000 species in the family a number have become pests by attacking the seed crops on which humans depend.

Perhaps the most important seed bug pests in North America are the chinch bugs of the genus *Blissus*. *Blissus leucopterus*, a very wide-spread species, is a particular problem. The adults overwinter in bunches of wild grasses, but on emerging in spring they then move into fields of cultivated crops such as wheat, barley, and other small-grained cereals. As these ripen and dry out, further generations of the bug move onto crops such as corn and

⊕ *A mating Neacoryphus ragweed fli Great Sm of Tenne seed bu wears "war"*

← *The small eastern milkweed bug, Lygaeus kalmii from the United States, feeds and lays its eggs on milkweed plants. The bug is immune to the toxic chemicals in milkweed but is itself toxic to other insect predators. Length 0.4–0.5 inches (10–13 mm). Trapezonotus arenarius is a less common species from the Northern Hemisphere, where it lives on savanna. Length 0.15–0.2 inches (4–5 mm).*

44 SEE ALSO Whiteflies 24:98, Aphids 24:100

Cross-references to relevant pages in this and other volumes

Easy-to-read and comprehensive text

extra information. At the bottom of many pages are cross-references to other articles of interest. They may be to related animals, animals that live in similar places, or that have similar behavior, predators (or prey), lifestyles, and much more. Each volume also contains a Set Index to the complete *World of Animals: Insects and Other Invertebrates*. Animals mentioned in the text are indexed by common and scientific name, and many topics are also covered. Since this set contains such a diverse group of animals, there are many unfamiliar words that need to be used. There is, therefore, a Glossary that will help you understand them. Each volume includes lists of useful Further Reading and Websites that help you take your research further.

Introductory article describes lesser groups, such as orders

Graphic full-color photographs bring text to life

Meticulous drawings illustrate details of structure and anatomy

Tables summarize classification of invertebrate groups and give scientific names of groups mentioned in the text

Who's Who tables summarize classification of each major group and give scientific names of animals mentioned in the text

Introductory article describes major groups of animals

At-a-glance boxes cover topics of special interest

Find the Animal

World of Animals: Insects and Other Invertebrates is the third part of a library that describes all groups of living animals. Each cluster of volumes in *World of Animals* will cover a familiar group of animals—mammals, birds, reptiles and amphibians, fish, and insects and other invertebrates.

The Animal Kingdon

The living world is divided into five kingdoms, one of which (kingdom Animalia) is the main subject of the *World of Animals*. Kingdom Animalia is divided into major groups called phyla, but only one of them (Chordata) contains those animals that have a backbone. Chordates, or vertebrates, include all the animals familiar to us and those most studied by scientists—mammals, birds, reptiles, amiphibians, and fish. There are about 38,000 species of vertebrates; but the animals without backbones (so-called invertebrates, such as insects, spiders, mollusks, and crustaceans) number at least 1 million species, probably many more. To find which set of volumes in the *World of Animals* you need, see the chart below.

Invertebrates in Particular

World of Animals: Insects and Other Invertebrates provides a broad survey of the most varied and numerous creatures on our planet. The only common factor linking all the animals described here is the lack of a backbone. We start by describing single-celled life forms (kingdom Protista), which are not regarded as true animals at all because the group includes both animal-like and plantlike forms and some that have both sets of characteristics.

There are 33 invertebrate phyla recognized here in the kingdom Animalia. Each one is quite distinct, so the diversity of animals described is immense. Mostly they are small, even microscopic; but monsters of the deep, such as the giant squid, can reach 65 feet (20 m) long.

Rank	Scientific name	Common name
Kingdom	Animalia	Animals
Phylum	Arthropoda	Animals with an external skeleton and jointed limbs
Class	Insecta	Six-legged arthropods
Order	Lepidoptera	Butterflies and moths
Family	Danaidae	Milkweed butterflies
Genus	*Danaus*	
Species	*Danaus plexppus*	

The kingdom Animalia is subdivided into phyla, classes, orders, families, genera, and species. Above is the classification for the monarch butterfly.

An important point must be made about the current scientific knowledge of these animals. New discoveries are being made every day, from the biology of individual creatures to the finding of new species. Knowledge is changing all the time, particularly regarding relationships between groups, and the number of species (and even phyla) increases all the time. Many of the figures given here are estimates based on the latest knowledge.

The greatest range of phyla is in Volume 21, where we describe single-celled life and 16 separate phyla of animals. The biggest phylum within the animal kingdom is the Arthropoda, which is made up of crustaceans, insects, spiders, and other familiar groups. They are covered in Volumes 22–29. Finally, there are the mainly marine phyla of mollusks and echinoderms in Volume 30.

⊖ *This chart lists the phyla in two of the five kingdoms. The phylum Arthropoda makes up a high proportion of all invertebrate animals.*

⊕ *The main groups of animals alive today. Volumes that cover each major group are indicated below.*

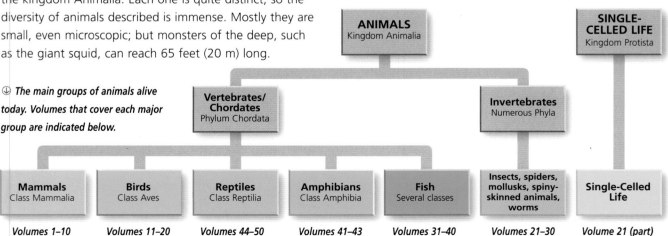

KINGDOM PROTISTA	single-celled animals
Phylum: Sarcomastigophora **(Vol. 21)**	flagellates, amebas
Phylum: Ciliophora **(Vol.21)**	ciliates
Phylum: Apicomplexa **(Vol. 21)**	malaria, etc.
Phylum: Microspora **(Vol. 21)**	single-celled parasites

KINGDOM ANIMALIA	animals
Phylum: Porifera **(Vol. 21)**	sponges
Phylum: Placozoa **(Vol. 21)**	plate animals
Phylum: Orthonectida **(Vol. 21)**	marine invertebrates
Phylum: Rhombozoa **(Vol. 21)**	parasitic invertebrates
Phylum: Cnidaria **(Vol. 21)**	jelly animals (hydrozoans, jellyfish, corals, and sea anemones)
Phylum: Ctenophora **(Vol. 21)**	comb jellies
Phylum: Gnathostomulida **(Vol. 21)**	no common name
Phylum: Gastrotricha **(Vol. 21)**	aquatic wormlike animals
Phylum: Rotifera **(Vol. 21)**	rotifers or wheel animalcules
Phylum: Acanthocephala **(Vol. 21)**	spiny-headed worms
Phylum: Cycliophora **(Vol. 21)**	microscopic animals
Phylum: Phoronida **(Vol. 21)**	horseshoe worms
Phylum: Bryozoa **(Vol. 21)**	moss animals

Phylum: Brachiopoda **(Vol. 21)**	lampshells
Phylum: Endoprocta **(Vol. 21)**	endoprocts
Phylum: Platyhelminthes **(Vol. 21)**	flatworms, tapeworms, and flukes
Phylum: Nemertea **(Vol. 21)**	ribbon worms
Phylum: Sipuncula **(Vol. 21)**	peanut worms
Phylum: Echiura **(Vol. 21)**	spoonworms
Phylum: Annelida **(Vol. 21)**	segmented worms
Phylum: Pogonophora **(Vol. 21)**	beard worms
Phylum: Kinorhyncha **(Vol. 21)**	spiny-crown worms
Phylum: Loricifera **(Vol. 21)**	loriciferans
Phylum: Nematoda **(Vol. 21)**	roundworms
Phylum: Nematomorpha **(Vol. 21)**	horsehair worms
Phylum: Priapulida **(Vol. 21)**	cactus worms
Phylum: Tardigrada **(Vol. 22)**	water bears
Phylum: Onychophora **(Vol. 22)**	velvet worms
Phylum: Arthropoda (Vols. 22–29)	jointed-limbed invertebrates
Phylum: Mollusca **(Vol. 30)**	mollusks, slugs, snails, etc.
Phylum: Echinodermata **(Vol. 30)**	echinoderms
Phylum: Chaetognatha **(Vol. 21)**	arrowworms
Phylum: Hemichordata **(Vol. 21)**	acorn worms

Phylum: Arthropoda

Subphylum: Pycnogonida **(Vol. 29)**	sea spiders
Subphylum: Chelicerata **(Vol. 29)**	spiders, scorpions, horseshoe crabs
Subphylum: Myriapoda **(Vol. 22)**	centipedes, millipedes, etc.
Subphylum: Crustacea **(Vol. 28)**	crustaceans
Subphylum: Hexapoda (Vol. 22)	Diplura, Protura, springtails, and insects

Subphylum: Hexapoda

Class: Collembola **(Vol. 22)**	springtails
Class: Protura **(Vol. 22)**	proturans
Class: Diplura **(Vol. 22)**	diplurans
Class: Insecta (Vols. 22–26)	insects

Class: Insecta

Order: Thysanura **(Vol. 22)**	silverfish
Order: Archeognatha **(Vol. 22)**	bristletails
Order: Ephemeroptera **(Vol. 22)**	mayflies
Order: Odonata **(Vol. 22)**	dragonflies and damselflies
Order: Phasmatodea **(Vol. 22)**	walkingsticks and leaf insects
Order: Dermaptera **(Vol. 22)**	earwigs
Order: Isoptera **(Vol. 22)**	termites
Order: Blattodea **(Vol. 22)**	cockroaches
Order: Mantodea **(Vol. 22)**	mantids
Order: Plecoptera **(Vol. 22)**	stoneflies
Order: Embioptera **(Vol. 22)**	web spinners
Order: Zoraptera **(Vol. 22)**	zorapterans
Order: Thysanoptera **(Vol. 22)**	thrips
Order: Psocoptera **(Vol. 22)**	booklice and barklice

Order: Phthiraptera **(Vol. 22)**	lice
Order: Neuroptera **(Vol. 22)**	lacewings
Order: Megaloptera **(Vol. 22)**	alderflies and dobsonflies
Order: Raphidioptera **(Vol. 22)**	snakeflies
Order: Trichoptera **(Vol. 22)**	caddisflies
Order: Mecoptera **(Vol. 22)**	scorpionflies and hangingflies
Order: Siphonaptera **(Vol. 22)**	fleas
Order: Strepsiptera **(Vol. 25)**	strepsipterans
Order: Orthoptera **(Vol. 23)**	crickets and grasshoppers
Order: Hemiptera **(Vol. 24)**	true bugs
Order: Coleoptera **(Vol. 25)**	beetles
Order: Diptera **(Vol. 23)**	flies
Order: Lepidoptera **(Vol. 26)**	butterflies and moths
Order: Hymenoptera **(Vol. 27)**	wasps, ants, bees, and sawflies

True Bugs

Before discussing bugs in detail, mention should first be made about the way in which the word "bug" is used. Biologists use the word bug to apply specifically to members of the order Hemiptera. Unfortunately, the word bug has now been adopted by most people to mean almost any kind of insect, which can be somewhat confusing. Also, in the past only members of the suborder Heteroptera were referred to as "true bugs." The rest, in the suborders Auchenorrhyncha and Sternorrhyncha, were termed "plant bugs," even though many hemipterans feed on plants. Here we use the word bug to refer to the "true bugs," that is, all of the insects in the order Hemiptera.

Whether they are plant feeders or feed on other insects, bugs are most easily seen on various kinds of vegetation or found in a net that has been dipped into a pond. Many of the plant feeders are associated with just a single food plant or a small range of plants and can easily

⊙ *A leaf-footed or flag-footed bug of the family Coreidae in rain forest in Peru, showing the typical wing arrangement of a heteropteran bug. The dark area at the rear is the overlap of the membranous forewings.*

Common name True bugs, bugs **Order** Hemiptera

MAIN FAMILIES

SUBORDER Heteroptera: 75 families, including:

Gerridae	Water striders
Veliidae	Ripple bugs
Hydrometridae	Water measurers
Nepidae	Water scorpions
Belostomatidae	Giant water bugs
Gelastocoridae	Toad bugs
Notonectidae	Backswimmers
Corixidae	Water boatmen
Tingidae	Lace bugs
Miridae	Plant bugs
Cimicidae	Bedbugs
Anthocoridae	Flower bugs
Nabidae	Damsel bugs
Reduviidae	Assassin bugs
Lygaeidae	Seed bugs
Pyrrhocoridae	Stainers
Alydidae	Broad-headed bugs
Coreidae	Leaf-footed bugs
Aradidae	Bark bugs
Berytidae	Stilt bugs
Rhopalidae	Scentless plant bugs
Pentatomidae	Stink bugs
Scutelleridae	Shield-backed bugs
Acanthosomatidae	Shield bugs

SUBORDER Auchenorrhyncha: 30 families, including:

Fulgoridae	Lanternflies
Cercopidae	Spittlebugs
Cicadidae	Cicadas
Cicadellidae	Leafhoppers
Membracidae	Treehoppers

SUBORDER Sternorrhyncha: 30 families, including:

Psyllidae	Jumping plant lice
Aleyrodidae	Whiteflies
Aphididae	Aphids
Coccidae	Scale insects
Pseudococcidae	Mealybugs

Number of species About 80,000 (9,800 U.S.)

Size From less than 0.04 in (1 mm) to about 6 in (15 cm)

Key features Mouthparts consist of a sucking proboscis (the rostrum) for feeding on plant sap or animal body fluids; most bugs have a pair of compound eyes, some have simple eyes (ocelli); most bugs have two pairs of wings, first pair may be leathery, second pair transparent and membranous, or both pairs may be membranous; wings may be absent altogether in some bugs; all bugs have a pair of antennae that can be short and not visible; metamorphosis incomplete (egg–nymphal stages–adult); in general, nymphal instars resemble adults, but are smaller and wingless

Diet Many bugs suck the sap from plants; others are predaceous, feeding on other arthropods; a few suck blood of vertebrates

Habitat Found in all habitats, including in and on fresh water; also beneath and on the sea

Distribution Worldwide

 SEE ALSO Cockroaches 22:68; Beetles 25:8

be found there. Many bug families contain plant-feeding species that are pests of cultivated plants. The predaceous species, however, are generally less restricted and are likely to be found searching for prey on almost any type of plant within their range of distribution. The parasitic species—including the human "lodger," the rather unpleasant bedbug—are usually to be found in or around the nests or homes of the animals on which they feed. While most bugs have no direct effect on humans, there is a group of tropical assassin bugs that not only suck human blood but also transmit disease.

Classification of the Hemiptera

In the earliest days of the classification of insects biologists recognized that the order Hemiptera could be divided into two distinct suborders, the Homoptera and the Heteroptera. In recent times, however, it has been discovered that the old suborder Homoptera contains two very distinct groups of bugs and should therefore be

discarded. As a result, the Hemiptera now includes the suborder Heteroptera as before, but the old Homoptera has been replaced by two suborders—the Auchenorrhyncha and the Sternorrhyncha. This should help the reader understand any earlier texts where the term Homoptera has been used.

Body Structure

Although there are three fairly distinct suborders of bugs, the group as a whole shares a number of features that separate them from the other insect orders. The body is subdivided into the normal three insect structures—the head, thorax, and abdomen—although in some families the divisions are not obvious. The most obvious structure that occurs in bugs is the rostrum, the sharp, sucking mouthparts with

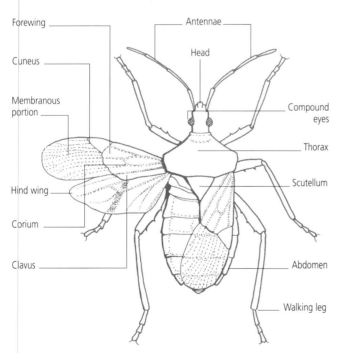

⊙ *The general body structure of a stink bug. As with most bugs, compound eyes are present, and the antennae have just a few segments. The pronotum covers the thorax above and extends back as a shield, the scutellum. The forewings of this heteropteran bug are typically divided into a leathery corium and cuneus, and a membranous hind portion.*

Labels (left, top to bottom): Forewing, Cuneus, Membranous portion, Hind wing, Corium, Clavus

Labels (right and center): Antennae, Head, Compound eyes, Thorax, Scutellum, Abdomen, Walking leg

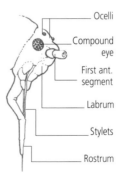

Sternorrhynchan head

Labels: Ocelli, Compound eye, First ant. segment, Labrum, Stylets, Rostrum

Auchenorrhynchan head

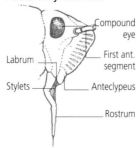

Labels: Compound eye, First ant. segment, Anteclypeus, Rostrum, Labrum, Stylets

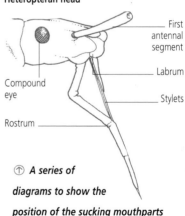

Heteropteran head

Labels: First antennal segment, Labrum, Stylets, Compound eye, Rostrum

⊙ *A series of diagrams to show the position of the sucking mouthparts on the heads of the three different bug suborders. The stylets, which cut into the food item and form the channel for sucking up the food, are clearly visible. The labrum could be thought of as equivalent to the upper lip.*

heteropterans it is situated well forward on the head, giving them a great deal of flexibility and allowing them to feed in a greater variety of ways than the other two groups. The most obvious visible differences between the Heteroptera and the other two suborders are the structure and arrangement of the wings: The forewings protect the hind wings and are held flat over the body, meeting along the centerline for part of their length, with an overlap on the hind section. The first area of the forewing, called the corium, is leathery and is the area that contains color pigments. The overlap on the hind section (the membrane) is thin and transparent, and very obviously separated from the corium by a distinct border. The hind wings are transparent and used for flying. Also noticeable

⟱ A seed bug, Spilostethus pandurus, feeds at a milkweed flower in the Kenyan savanna. It is warningly colored, suggesting that it is distasteful, perhaps from taking up poisons from the milkweed plant.

which they pierce plants or the bodies of animals in order to feed. Most bug species have a pair of compound eyes, but they may be absent in some of the highly adapted plant feeders. Some of the bug families have simple eyes (ocelli), while others have no eyes at all. All bugs have a pair of antennae, although in some species they may be very short and difficult to spot.

The thorax, as in other insects, has a pair of walking legs on each of its three segments as well as a pair of wings on each of the second and third segments. In a few families there may be just a single pair of wings, or they may be absent altogether, at least in the females. The abdomen is typical of an insect (as shown in the diagram opposite), and only in a few families does it bear any special structures visible to the naked eye.

The Heteroptera

A major structural difference—but one that is not easily visible—between the Heteroptera and the other two suborders is the position of the rostrum. In the

on these bugs are the well-developed pronotum covering the thorax, and the shield-shaped scutellum. The scutellum extends over the abdomen behind the pronotum but is part of the thorax. In any of the heteropteran families forms may exist with either full-length wings, wings that only cover part of the abdomen, or wings that are reduced to tiny stumps and are hardly visible.

The Auchenorrhyncha

The Auchenorrhyncha is the suborder whose members are most likely to be confused with the Heteroptera, at least at first sight. However, closer examination shows that the rostrum rises from beneath and the back of the head, so that it can only point downward or backward. The forewings are colored, and they cover the transparent hind wings but never have an overlapping transparent area. In cicadas both sets of wings are transparent. Adults of the suborder always have three segments making up the tarsus of each leg.

The Sternorrhyncha

The only family in the suborder Sternorrhyncha that is likely to be mistaken for members of the other two suborders is the Psyllidae, the jumping plant lice. They bear a resemblance to tiny cicadas. Otherwise, the Sternorrhyncha are not immediately recognizable as bugs; in fact, some of them do not seem to resemble insects in any way at all. In all families in the Sternorrhyncha the rostrum appears to emerge from the thorax between the front legs. In reality it sticks out far back on the head, allowing them even less movement than bugs in the Auchenorrhyncha. In families in which wings are present, both pairs are transparent. Adults have just two segments making up the tarsus of each leg.

Feeding Apparatus

All bugs have a rostrum with which they suck up their liquid food, either sap, the body fluids of other insects and spiders, or the blood of vertebrates. Although the rostrum is a tubular structure varying in length, it has the same arrangement of structures as in the biting mouthparts of other insects such as beetles and cockroaches: The mandibles and maxillae, instead of being broad, flat, and pincerlike, are long and thin. In this form they are referred to as stylets.

The mandibles have sawlike ends that are used to cut into the stems of plants or the bodies of insect prey and to pierce the skin of vertebrate hosts. The maxillae are pushed into the hole made by the mandibles. The maxillae are long and thin, with grooves along their inner edges. When the two maxillae are held together side by side, the grooves form two tubes. One tube is used to squirt saliva onto the food, the other to suck up the food. Both the mandibles and maxillae lie inside a tube formed by the labium, the lower "lip" of chewing insects, which keeps the delicate structures protected when not in use. The outer tube is not pushed with the maxillae into the hole made by the mandibles but remains outside. The way in which the outer tube remains outside varies according to suborder and family.

In a number of predaceous families in the Heteroptera the prey is held by the bug's front legs while its juices are sucked out. In others, especially if the prey is soft bodied like a caterpillar, it is held on the end of the rostrum. Plant-sucking bugs of all three suborders normally pierce the phloem, the tubes in plants through which foods manufactured by photosynthesis flow. A few of the very small species, however, suck out the contents of single cells.

Honeydew

Bugs that are members of the Auchenorrhyncha and Sternorrhyncha feed only on plant sap, which can come from the phloem vessels, the xylem (water-carrying) vessels, or from single cells, depending on the species. Sap is a very dilute solution containing a range of food substances—including sugars, amino acids, vitamins, and salts—which the bug needs in order to grow. Sap contains proportionally much more water and sugar than amino acids. In order for the bugs to obtain enough amino acids to build their body proteins, they have to get

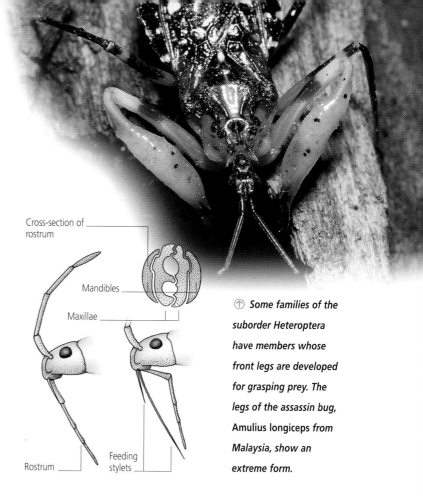

⬆ *Some families of the suborder Heteroptera have members whose front legs are developed for grasping prey. The legs of the assassin bug,* Amulius longiceps *from Malaysia, show an extreme form.*

⬆ *The typical mouthparts of bugs, with the segmented, movable rostrum. The cross-section shows the tubes formed by the mandibles and maxillae and used to suck up food and squirt out saliva.*

rid of all the excess sugar and water. They do that by passing it out of the anus as a dilute sugar solution known as honeydew. Where very large numbers of bugs such as aphids are feeding from trees, the honeydew can fall almost like rain onto the ground below. The honeydew is a favorite food of many ants and some bees.

Life Cycle and Development

In common with the orders Orthoptera (crickets and grasshoppers), Blattodea (cockroaches), and Mantodea (mantids), bugs in the Hemiptera have a life cycle that passes from the egg through a series of instars to the adult form. Each stage of development up to the adult form is called a nymph. The shape and structure of bug eggs vary greatly, but members of the same family tend to have similar-looking eggs. Some eggs are smooth; others have a sculptured surface or have spikes or longer projections. Eggs may be laid singly or in batches.

⤒ These lupin aphids, Macrosiphum albifrons from Europe, are wingless females that reproduce by parthenogenesis. The upper female is just giving birth to a shiny, green youngster.

In three bug families—the leaf-footed bugs (Coreidae), the shield bugs (Acanthosomatidae), and the aphids (Aphididae)—the first instar nymph possesses an "egg-burster," a "t"-shaped tooth that helps it escape from the eggshell. The tooth is shed with the first instar skin when it is molted. In most bugs what hatches from the egg looks like a miniature, wingless adult, but with some differences. (The exceptions to the general rule, mainly in some of the Sternorrhyncha, are dealt with in the entries for the separate families.) The most obvious differences are the total lack of wings and the fact that the head is much larger in relation to the rest of the body when compared to the adult bug. Also, sometimes —but not always —the bug nymphs may be a totally different color or pattern than the adults. The nymphs have fewer segments making up the tarsi on the legs and fewer segments on the antennae than the adults, but these differences are less obvious.

Each nymph feeds until fully grown, when it molts its skin to become the next instar. In the Heteroptera there are six instars including the adult stage, whereas in the other two suborders there is more variation. In the aphids, for example, there may be either four or five instars. The highest number of recorded instars is in a species of cicada, which has seven. There may even be a difference between the sexes in the scale insects. With each successive instar the bug's body gradually gets larger in relation to the head; by the third instar tiny wing buds are usually just visible and become obvious by the fourth instar. The stage from the final instar to the adult form brings about the greatest change, with all body structures becoming fully developed. After casting off the fifth instar skin, the newly hatched adult has to expand both sets of wings to their full extent before they dry off; otherwise they will not be properly formed and will be useless.

Defense Mechanisms and Behaviors

As in all insects, bugs have many enemies. They therefore need some defenses against attackers. Camouflage is an obvious one, and many bugs are cryptically colored in order to blend in with the background. Of course, they must also have the ability to keep still, since the slightest movement would soon give them away. Many of the

⤺ A male Rhinocoris albopilosus assassin bug from Uganda guards a female while she lays eggs. She is almost certainly his mate, and he is preventing other males from attempting to mate with her.

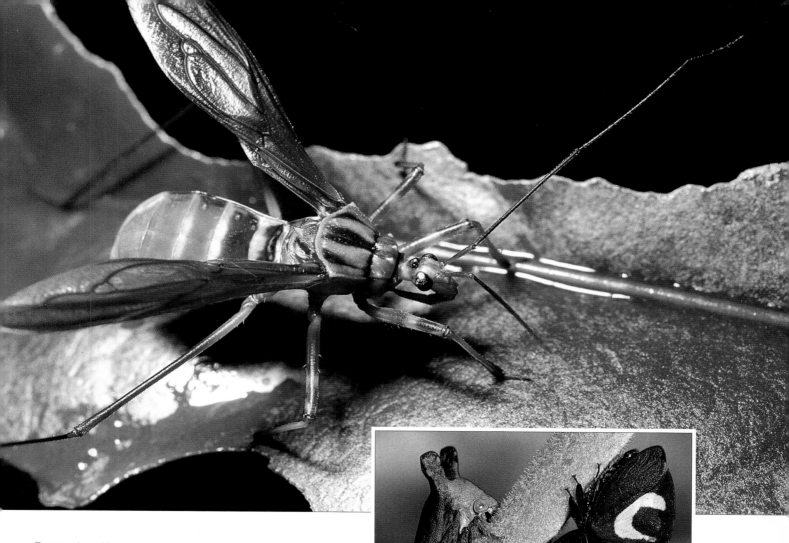

↑ *A number of bugs are mimics of social wasps, which tend to be avoided by predators because of their sting. A beautiful example of such mimicry is seen in this* Sphodrolestes *species assassin bug.*

→ *Two species of treehopper from Brazil employ different means of defense. The black-and-white bugs,* Membracis foliata, *use warning coloration, while the green bug uses camouflage.*

Sternorrhyncha, especially the nymphs, cover themselves in a layer of wax or produce waxy strands or powder so that they do not look like insects at all. The wax also keeps them from drying out and is to some extent a form of protection against parasitic insects such as wasps. Some bugs are effectively hidden from searching eyes by their resemblance to leaves or thorns.

Bright colors often give a warning message, which to a vertebrate predator such as a bird means "Keep off, I'm unpleasant." That is in fact true, since members of the Heteroptera have various glands that produce unpleasant chemicals to deter attackers. Other bugs are known to take in the poisons from the plants on which they feed. The poisons have no apparent effect on the bug but can make any predator that feeds on them very ill.

Structural defenses include spines that make it difficult for a predator to grasp the bug, detachable legs that break off in a predator's mouth enabling the bug to escape, and "armor plating" such as the thick cuticle of many shield bugs. Two groups of bugs can even go on the offensive: Both the backswimmers and many of the larger assassin bugs can plunge their sharp rostrum into an attacker, even a human. They are capable of delivering a very painful bite if handled carelessly.

Water Striders Gerridae

Common water strider (Gerris lacustris)

Common name Water
striders
(pondskaters)

Family Gerridae

Suborder Heteroptera

Order Hemiptera

Number of species About 500 (45 U.S.)

Size From about 0.2 in (5 mm) to 0.7 in (18 mm)

Key features Male usually smaller than female; middle
and hind legs much longer than body and
splayed out sideways for skating on water;
middle legs closer to hind legs than to front
legs; front legs adapted for grasping prey;
body oval to elongate, covered in dense layer
of "hairs" that prevent it from becoming wet;
wings may be full, partial, or absent; eyes
large

Habits Skating around on the surface of water in
search of prey

Breeding Once he has found a mate, the male usually
stays on the female's back; eggs laid on
floating plants or among debris

Diet Small insects that have fallen on the water,
small fish, tadpoles; some cannibalism of
nymphs is recorded; prey often shared

Habitat All types of freshwater habitat such as ponds,
lakes, streams, rivers, canals, and animal
water troughs, but excluding very fast-moving
water; also the surface of the sea

Distribution Worldwide for freshwater species; some
Halobates species are oceanic

⤒ *The common water strider, Gerris lacustris, can be found
on almost any stretch of still, fresh water. The bugs use their
hind two pairs of legs to move across the water, leaving the
short front legs free to catch food. Length 0.3 inches (8 mm).*

*Water striders are amazing bugs, perfectly
adapted to stand on the surface film of
the water with their water-repellent
legs. They can locate prey and possible
mates by the movement of ripples
on the water's surface.*

THE QUESTION EVERYONE ASKS when they see a
water strider darting across the surface of a
stretch of water is "How do they do that?" The
answer is, of course, that the bugs are highly
modified for their rather special lifestyle.

Special Wetsuits

The bug's body is covered in a thick coating of
hairs that do not get wet. Therefore, even when
in contact with water, the bug does not
become waterlogged and sink. The legs are also
impossible to make wet, with the exception of
the very ends of the tarsi, which appear to
pierce the surface film of water. Close
examination reveals that the end of each leg
stands inside a tiny dimple in the surface of the
water. By pushing against the dimples with the
middle legs and steering with the hind pair, the
bug is able to scoot across the surface. If it is in
danger, however, the bug can skip across the
surface in a series of rapid jumps.

Feeding on Misfortune

Water striders, at least those that live on fresh
water, feed mainly on insects that have fallen in
and are struggling in the surface film. The
movement of the insect sends out ripples across
the water surface which the bug detects,
allowing it to home in on the insect. Water
striders have large eyes in relation to their body
size, which suggests that sight is important in
the final approach and for pouncing on prey.
The bug seizes the prey with its front pair of
legs and then pierces it with the sharp rostrum.

Drowning insects are not their only prey:
The bugs are also able to detect ripples

⊙ *Feeding on a
drowning damselfly that
has become trapped in
the surface film of a
pond are three Gerris
odontogaster toothed
pondskaters from
Europe. Their appearance
is typical of the family as
a whole.*

produced by small fish
and tadpoles swimming close to
the surface, and can catch them as a
result. Water striders seem to have no
problem with sharing their food. As many as
10 individuals of the British toothed pondskater,
Gerris odontogaster, may cluster around and
feed at larger prey such as a damselfly.

Using surface ripples to detect struggling
prey is not the only way in which water striders
make use of such signals. They have also been
found to be used by some species for activities
like attracting a mate, conducting courtship,
identifying the sex of an individual, guarding a
mate, stimulating egg laying, and indicating a
territory. For example, males and females of
Rhagadotarsus species striders in Australia use
their legs to produce patterns of ripples to
communicate with each other. This may happen
while they are holding onto some suitable
object in the water, which then becomes a focal
point for mating and egg laying. The males
have also been shown to signal in a way that
stimulates the females to lay their eggs.

A Life on the Ocean Waves

The oceans are very hostile places for small creatures, but five of
the 40 or so known *Halobates* species striders have overcome the
problem. They spend their entire lives on tropical oceans, often
hundreds of miles from the nearest dry land. As a result, not a great
deal is known about them. They are typical gerrids: The male is
smaller than the female, and their life cycle is that of a typical bug. In
order to start the cycle, the females have to find something on the
water surface, such as floating seashells, bits of wood, or even bird
feathers, on which to lay their eggs.

The eggs are large in relation to the size of the female, which
presumably means that the first instars are also large and get a good
start in life under difficult conditions. The individuals that have been
observed have been seen to feed on dead jellyfish, floating fish eggs,
small fish, and other small creatures such as crustaceans swimming
near the surface.

European water
cricket (*Velia caprai*)

Common name Ripple bugs (water crickets,
small water striders)

Family Veliidae

Suborder Heteroptera

Order Hemiptera

Number of species About 420 (35 U.S.)

Size From about 0.06 in (1.5 mm) to 0.35 in
(9 mm)

Key features Resemble water striders but in general are
smaller and more heavily built; middle and
hind legs splayed out for skating on water
surface; legs not much longer than body;
middle legs halfway between fore- and hind
legs; wings long, short, or absent

Habits Found skating around on the surface of water
in search of prey

Breeding Females lay eggs among vegetation

Diet Small, drowning insects; small water
organisms; mosquito eggs

Habitat All types of freshwater habitat including
ponds, lakes, streams (even fast-running),
rivers, and canals; water trapped in plants in
tropical forests; coastal saltwater pools

Distribution Worldwide, but most common in tropical
America and tropical Asia

⏚ *Velia caprai, the European water cricket, is well adapted
to skate across the water with its splayed-out legs and
water-repellent feet. It feeds on small invertebrates that fall
onto the water and possibly mosquito larvae under the
water. Length 0.2–0.3 inches (5–8 mm).*

Ripple Bugs

Veliidae

*The family Veliidae includes the tiniest bugs in
the Heteroptera—some no bigger than the head
of a match. They are remarkable for their ability
to propel themselves rapidly across the water
away from danger.*

RIPPLE BUGS ARE AMAZING creatures: If they sense
danger, they use a form of "jet propulsion" to
escape. They simply release a droplet of saliva
onto the surface of the water in the direction
they want to head. The surface tension of the
water in front is lowered, and the bug shoots
forward across the surface to safety.

For normal movement ripple bugs use
their legs to skate, walk, or run around on
the surface. However, they can also be found
walking along the banks of the slow-flowing
water courses on which most of the species live.
At first glance they may be mistaken for water
striders, but in ripple bugs all three pairs of legs
are equally spaced along the thorax, and the
hind two pairs are of similar length.

Strong Swimmers

A few species, such as *Rhagovelia* from North
America, live on fast-flowing waters and have
special modifications on the tarsi of the middle
legs to help them against the strength of the
current. On the last tarsal segment are
structures called swimming fans, made up of
special blades or tufts of hairs that normally lie
flat in slots on the tarsus. When the middle legs
are pushed back during a swimming stroke, the
fans open up to form a paddle, just like a duck's
webbed foot, allowing the bug to swim against
the strong current.

Some species are fully winged; others can
have both short-winged and wingless forms.
North American and European *Velia* species can
have white and brownish-orange markings to
brighten up their rather dull body color.

Ripple bugs are often found in quite large
groups, the numbers in a group relating to the

⏚ *Velia caprai, the
European water cricket,
lives on slow-moving
waters, where it may
often be found in quite
large aggregations.
Although, like this
individual, it usually has
reduced wings,
occasional fully winged
adults are produced.*

speed of the water current: Where the water is still, large numbers may be found together; but (for an unknown reason) as the water current speeds up, the distance between the bugs increases. They feed on small insects that have fallen into the water, small water-dwelling crustaceans, insect larvae, and the eggs of aquatic insects. In some species, as with the water striders, larger prey may be shared with other individuals. The ripple bug may not be so generous if it is only feeding on small prey.

Among the *Microvelia* species are some of the tiniest of the Heteroptera, few of them exceeding 0.08 inches (2 mm) in length. Most lack wings in both sexes. While many are found on fresh water, quite a few species are coastal—some inhabit the holes dug in coastal mud by various land crabs. *Microvelia leucotheca* has been found on mudflats and mangrove swamps in Colombia, where it runs over the mud at low tide in search of prey.

Water Measurers

Although related to the ripple bugs, the water measurers in the family Hydrometridae look totally different. They are very long, thin bugs, with a very long head and a pair of bulging eyes. Their legs are also long and thin, and the overall impression they give is of a small stick insect or a walkingstick. Most species have either very short wings or lack them altogether. Rather than skating on the water surface like the water striders and ripple bugs, they walk around in a more sedate manner. They can also be found walking on surface vegetation or on the banks of ponds and slow-moving water courses. Their main source of food is tiny insect larvae and crustaceans that swim close to the surface. The bugs catch them by plunging their rostrum down through the water surface and into the prey below, which they are able to detect by its swimming movements. Water measurers also take small insects trapped on the water surface, provided they are no longer struggling.

What at first sight seems to be a small walkingstick is in fact a water measurer, Hydrometra stagnorum, making its way across the vegetation on the surface of a garden pond in England.

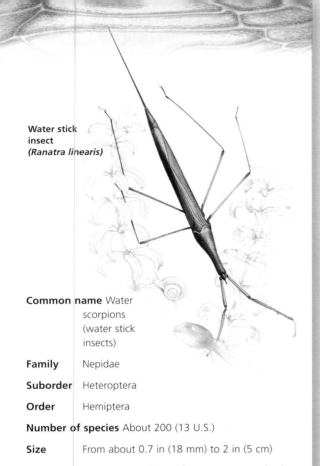

Water stick
insect
(*Ranatra linearis*)

Common name	Water scorpions (water stick insects)
Family	Nepidae
Suborder	Heteroptera
Order	Hemiptera
Number of species	About 200 (13 U.S.)
Size	From about 0.7 in (18 mm) to 2 in (5 cm)
Key features	Front legs adapted for grasping prey; body flattened and oval or long and sticklike; fully winged and capable of flight; a long, thin breathing tube extends from the hind end
Habits	Walk around on vegetation beneath the water hunting for prey; may hang below surface with breathing tube just above surface, taking in air
Breeding	Eggs laid inside aquatic plants; males of some species use their front legs to grasp the female during mating
Diet	Insect larvae, tadpoles, and small crustaceans such as water fleas
Habitat	Still and slow-moving water of ponds, lakes, canals, and rivers
Distribution	Worldwide in suitable habitats, especially in tropical regions

⤒ *The water stick insect,* Ranatra linearis, *hangs from the surface by its breathing siphon and waits to catch prey such as water fleas with its front legs. It is not a good swimmer and mostly crawls among the weeds. Length (without siphon) 1 inch (2.5 cm).*

Water Scorpions   Nepidae

The resemblance of water scorpions to the more dangerous scorpions of the arachnid world is a little misleading. Although the breathing tube sticking out of the end of the abdomen looks like it could sting—and their pincerlike appendages can deliver a sharp stab—they are of no real danger.

THE COMMON NAME OF water scorpion is perhaps a poor one, since members of the family vary in appearance: Some resemble stick insects or walkingsticks, while others are shaped more like a short, fat, pointed surfboard—neither of which are like scorpions at all.

Breathing Tubes

There are two features shared by all water scorpions. They bear a pair of grasping front legs and a breathing tube on the rear end of the abdomen. The tube is made up of two half tubes lying side by side to form a complete one. It is pushed up above the water so that the bug can breathe as it hangs just below the surface while waiting for passing prey, such as tadpoles, small fish, and insect larvae. In North American and European species the breathing tube is shorter than the combined length of the head, thorax, and abdomen; in South African *Laccotrephe* species, however, it can be more than twice the length.

Water scorpions are poor swimmers—instead, they walk stealthily around on vegetation beneath the water. If threatened, they will lie absolutely still and pretend to be dead.

⊝ *A water scorpion,* Nepa cinerea *from Europe, hangs motionless in the water waiting to grasp any suitable passing prey in its specially adapted front legs.*

⊝ **Hydrocyrius columbiae** *from Uganda is one of the world's largest giant water bugs. It inhabits large lakes and is seldom seen except when it comes to lights at night, which it does in large numbers.*

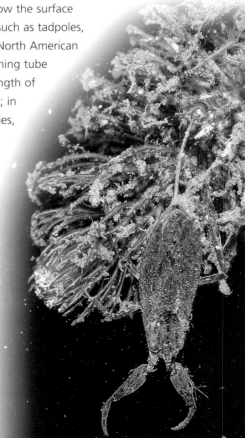

Giant Water Bugs

The giant water bugs in the family Belostomatidae are quite impressive creatures. Not only are they the largest of all bugs, reaching a size of 2.4 inches (6 cm), but they are also among the largest of insects. In shape they are similar to the broad-bodied water scorpions, but they do not have a breathing tube extending from the rear end. Unlike the water scorpions, the giant water bugs are active swimmers. Accordingly, their hind legs are fringed with hairs to form effective paddles. The grasping front legs are heavily built and powerful, and the rostrum is stout and very sharp. The giant water bugs can deliver an extremely painful bite if they are handled carelessly. In North America they have the common name of "toe-biters," since they will stab into a foot if trodden on beneath the water. They are perhaps more likely to be seen out of water, since they are strong fliers and are attracted to bright lights at night. In North America that habit has earned them another common name of "electric-light bug." In a number of Asian countries people exploit the tendency of the bug to fly toward light.

Bright lights are set up to attract the bugs, which are then collected, cooked, and eaten.

Females of many species lay their eggs on the bottom surface or among water plants, but perhaps the most fascinating characteristic of some species is that the males look after the eggs until they hatch. Parental care is found in the males of both *Belostoma* species and *Abedus* species in North America. For example, after they have mated and their eggs have been fertilized, *Abedus herberti* females seek out another male of their own species. They then proceed to lay their eggs on the new male's back before deserting them completely. The male takes great care of his batch of eggs until they hatch. He ensures that the eggs remain wet at all times, but he also exposes them to the air at regular intervals. When submerged, he maintains a flow of water over the eggs by rocking his body back and forth. If the eggs are removed from his back—even if they are kept damp and well oxygenated—they will fail to hatch, proving that his parenting skills are highly effective.

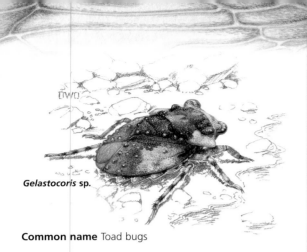

Gelastocoris sp.

Common name Toad bugs

Family Gelastocoridae

Suborder Heteroptera

Order Hemiptera

Number of species About 150 (7 U.S.)

Size From about 0.2 in (5 mm) to 0.5 in (13 mm)

Key features Body oval, short, and squat; rather warty in appearance, like a toad; head quite flat and broad with large, bulging eyes; front legs modified for catching prey; other legs are used to hop along like toads; well camouflaged, usually resembling pebbles

Habits Not very active, but will pounce on any small, suitable prey; adults may swim to avoid danger, but rarely fly

Breeding Eggs are laid into the ground

Diet Mainly small insects

Habitat Along sides of ponds, lakes, and streams; also in decaying wood and under leaves and stones away from water

Distribution Worldwide, but commoner in tropical regions

⤴ *The various* Gelastocoris *species of toad bugs from the United States demonstrate clearly the close resemblance of the bug to the real toad, with its large, bulging eyes and "warty" body. However, when still, they are well camouflaged and resemble small stones. Length 0.3–0.4 inches (7–10 mm).*

Toad Bugs

Gelastocoridae

Toad bugs owe their common name to their hopping motion and their habit of seeking insect prey by the edges of rivers, lakes, and ponds. At first sight it is easy to mistake them for baby toads; at rest they resemble small, rough pebbles.

TOAD BUGS ARE ALMOST as broad as they are long, and overall they have a rather warty appearance, much like that of a real toad. The head does not extend very far forward from the pronotum, and the most noticeable thing about it is the size of the bulging eyes—they stick out sideways rather like those of a chameleon. The antennae, however, are tiny and are completely hidden beneath the large eyes.

Toad bugs are predaceous, feeding on small insects. In species that live near water the prey is taken from the water's edge, while terrestrial species find their prey on the ground. Adults and nymphs move mainly by hopping, jumping on suitable prey when they come across it. The front femurs are very large and contain the strong muscles that are used to hold onto the prey. Once they have captured their prey, they hold it in their grasping front legs to subdue it and then feed on it. Although the adults are fully winged, it appears that they seldom, if ever, fly.

The female bugs lay their eggs in mud, sand, soil, or under stones. It is reported that toad bugs jump into shallow water and swim to safety if they are attacked.

⬅ *A* Nerthra *species toad bug nymph seen here in Nepal has its back camouflaged with sand.*

Shore Bugs

The family Saldidae (the shore bugs) has about 260 species with a worldwide distribution. They live in the same type of habitat as the toad bugs, but they are smaller and probably end up being eaten by them on occasion. Fortunately, they are very quick, jumping rapidly into the air and taking flight when attacked.

Shore bugs vary between 0.08 inches (2 mm) and 0.2 inches (5 mm) in length. They are generally oval and slightly elongate in shape when viewed from above. Being hunters, they have large, bulging eyes, and the male has a roughened area on the side of the abdomen that helps him hold onto the female during mating. Shore bugs live along the shores of both still water sources (including garden ponds) and running water. They can also be found on the shores of estuaries and on the main seashore between the tides. A few species live away from water in dry habitats. The estuarine species hang onto water plants while the tide is in and can only last for two or three hours under water. All members of the family are predaceous, feeding mainly on small arthropods.

The marine bug, *Aepophilus bonnairei*, is found along the Atlantic coast from the British Isles down to Morocco in northern Africa. It spends its entire life on the lower shore, living in rock crevices, where it lies submerged while the tide is in. It has no ocelli, and the wings are greatly reduced in size. Little is known about its feeding habits; but since it is tiny—around 0.1 inches (3 mm) long on average—its prey is presumably tiny also. The bugs are subsocial, meaning that they live in colonies in which the females look after the eggs and care for the young until they become adult. They are found in what are probably family groups, one female surrounded by a number of nymphs, which are her offspring.

⊕ **Gelastocoris peruensis** *from Peru is a typical toad bug. It is sitting at the edge of a lake where it resembles the stones that surround it, making it difficult for a predator to spot.*

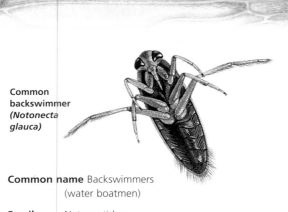

Common
backswimmer
(*Notonecta
glauca*)

Common name Backswimmers
(water boatmen)

Family Notonectidae

Suborder Heteroptera

Order Hemiptera

Number of species About 300 (35 U.S.)

Size From about 0.2 in (5 mm) to 0.6 in (15 mm)

Key features Body boat shaped, flat on the underside; usually hang head down from water surface, showing underside; eyes large; ears present in both sexes; rostrum strong and sharp; front legs used to grasp prey; hind legs long, fringed with hairs and used as paddles; wings well developed; underside of abdomen bears water-repellent hairs

Habits All species are strong swimmers, coming to the surface regularly to replenish air supply; also strong fliers, moving from one area of water to another

Breeding In some species males stridulate to attract females; eggs attached to objects in the water, such as stones or plants

Diet Aquatic animals including insect larvae, tadpoles, and small fish as well as insects that have fallen into the water

Habitat Lakes and ponds, water tanks, and animal water troughs

Distribution Worldwide

⊙ *The common backswimmer,* Notonecta glauca, *is widespread throughout Europe and lives in ponds, ditches, and canals. It swims upside down, propelled by two long legs that paddle like oars, making it look like a rowboat. Length up to 0.8 inches (20 mm).*

Backswimmers Notonectidae

Backswimmers are well named for their habit of swimming upside down with their undersides pointing toward the water surface. The large eyes, located near the top of the head, are therefore able to look down into the water as the bug searches for suitable prey.

LOOKING DOWN INTO A POND, it can be quite difficult to pick out backswimmers as they hang upside down just beneath the water surface because their general coloring matches that of the pond. Their camouflage colors presumably hide them quite well from any water birds on the lookout for an easy meal. Their upper side, on the other hand, is pale, which means that they blend into the background of the sky when viewed from beneath, probably making them more difficult for a fish to spot.

They are efficient killers, easily immobilizing prey smaller or even bigger than themselves by stabbing it with their sharp, powerful rostrum. Digestive juices are injected into the prey through the rostrum, and the liquid contents of its body are then sucked out. As with bugs in

⊙ *A North American species of backswimmer from Arizona hangs motionless at the water surface while it refreshes its air supply.*

⊙ *The common backswimmer,* Notonecta glauca *from Europe, shows two important lifestyle adaptations. The paddle-shaped hind legs used for swimming have rows of hairs along them to increase their surface area. The large eyes are of importance in spotting prey in the murky water in which it often lives.*

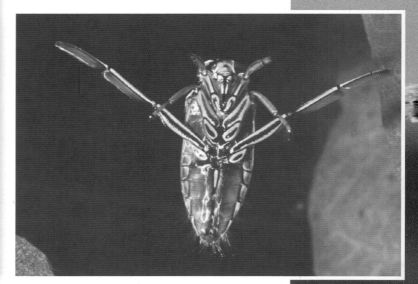

other families, backswimmers can deliver a painful jab to a human finger if they are picked up carelessly. In order to study their upper sides, it is best to restrict them in a small glass tube where they may be examined without the observer coming to any harm. Not all backswimmers hunt below the water—some specialize on insects that have fallen into the water and are struggling on the surface. The backswimmers have the ability to detect the difference between ripples in the water produced by prey and ripples produced by individuals of their own species. They are strong fliers, enabling them to move from pond to pond; they can also literally jump out of the water and immediately take flight.

Despite the fact that they live under the water, both sexes have ears, and the males of many species stridulate. They produce sounds attractive to females by rubbing rough areas of the front legs against the rostrum. In some backswimmers the bubble of air held under the wings acts as an amplifier for the sounds. For example, it appears that the sounds produced by a number of *Buenoa* species males can be heard from several yards away. They start with a series of clicks; but as they get closer to the female, it turns into a rapid hum.

The life cycle of *Notonecta* species, which are found all over the world, is quite typical of the family as a whole. Once mating has taken place, the female lays her eggs in or on various pondweeds. The female of *N. glauca* from Europe is able to use her ovipositor to cut into plant stems where she lays her elongate eggs. Like their parents, all nymphal stages are active predators, catching suitable-sized prey and in some cases eating one another. While land-dwelling insects take in air to expand their body after they have molted, aquatic bugs either swallow water or take it in through their body surface in order to expand into their new skin. Depending on the species and the water

⇑ *The common water boatman or common backswimmer,* Notonecta glauca *from Europe, hangs onto submerged vegetation while waiting to pounce on passing prey items.*

temperature in a particular year, there may be one or two generations produced annually. When looking down into water where backswimmers live, it is not uncommon to find both adults and nymphs of all stages present at the same time.

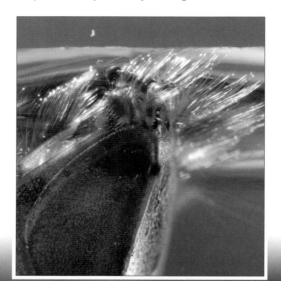

⊖ ⇩ *Right: This closeup of the end of the abdomen of a backswimmer shows some of the bristles that hold the bubble of air. Below: A common backswimmer,* Notonecta glauca, *hangs at the water surface with its underside in contact with the atmosphere. It is changing the bubble of air that it uses to breathe beneath the water, and that is trapped in rows of bristles beneath the abdomen.*

Bubbles of Life

It is interesting to note how backswimmers and other water bugs manage to obtain the oxygen they need. They do so by coming to the surface of the water at intervals to take on new air supplies. The air is trapped as a bubble under rows of water-repellent hairs on the underside of the abdomen in both nymphs and adults. Adults, being bigger, can hold onto an even larger quantity of air by trapping some between the wings and the top of the abdomen. The insect takes oxygen from the bubble as required through the spiracles. At the same rate as the oxygen is used, more enters the bubble from the surrounding water to replace it. Provided the bug is not too active, the slow removal of oxygen and the replacement from the water will keep it breathing quite happily. While its activity levels are low, it can remain beneath the water for as long as six hours without having to replace the bubble. If the bug is very active, however, or if the water is low in oxygen—for example, in warm weather—the insect has to make regular trips to the surface for fresh supplies of air. A second reason why the bubble may need changing regularly is that it contains nitrogen as well as oxygen. (Nitrogen makes up about four-fifths of the earth's atmosphere.)

Lesser Water Boatmen

Bugs in the family Corixidae are called lesser water boatmen because the members of the Notonectidae (backswimmers) are sometimes referred to as water boatmen. Clearly, both live in water, but it is not too difficult to distinguish them from one another. Instead of swimming on their backs, lesser water boatmen swim on their fronts so that the top of the body is always visible to the observer. The upper side of the body is flatter than in the backswimmers but still rounded, and all three pairs of legs are different from one another. The hind legs are the largest; they are flattened, with fringes of hairs, and are used for swimming. The middle legs are similar in length to the hind legs, but are slim and used for holding onto weeds and other objects in the water. The front legs are short and in the majority of the family are used for gathering food. The tarsus of each front leg has only one segment, along which is a fringe of tough bristles. The bristles are used to scoop up and filter out tiny algae, diatoms, and tiny animals on which the bugs feed. Males of some species also use the scoops on the front legs to hold onto the females during mating.

A few species in the family are predators. *Cymatia coleoptrata*, a European species, lives in pools where it rests among plants beneath the water. It will swim out and catch small water crustaceans, insect larvae, and even nymphs of other water boatmen, holding the prey in its front legs as it feeds. *Glaencorisa* species have similar habits but are large-eyed and nocturnal. They have long hairs on their front legs which they use as a type of net to catch small crustaceans and other small water creatures on which they feed.

Corixa punctata, the lesser water boatman, is commonly found in weedy ponds and lakes where it feeds on algae and detritus on the bottom. As well as being powerful swimmers, these bugs can fly.

The nitrogen in the bubble slowly dissolves into the water, and the bubble gradually shrinks in size. The smaller the bubble, the less oxygen it can take in from the water and the less use it is. As it shrinks, it eventually has to be replaced.

In *Notonecta* species, having taken on a bubble of air, the bugs swim down and hold onto water plants or other objects to prevent themselves from floating back to the surface. *Buenoa* species backswimmers from the warm temperate and tropical regions of the Old World and *Anisops* species from the temperate and tropical regions of the New World, however, are able to hang still in the water, unaided, at any depth they wish. They manage this by taking on a much smaller bubble of air and therefore becoming less buoyant than

Notonecta, so they do not float upward. This means that they have a smaller supply of oxygen available to them. To overcome the problem, their body contains stocks of hemoglobin—the substance that carries oxygen in the blood. The bugs can store a certain amount of oxygen in the hemoglobin to use when submerged. They do not have to come to the surface as often as would be expected with such a small bubble of air. In addition, the presence of hemoglobin means that they are able to live in water that is low in oxygen.

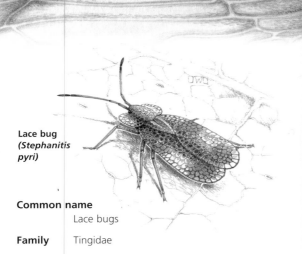

Lace bug (*Stephanitis pyri*)

Common name
Lace bugs

Family Tingidae

Suborder Heteroptera

Order Hemiptera

Number of species About 1,800 (157 U.S.)

Size From about 0.08 in (2 mm) to 0.2 in (5 mm)

Key features Body flattened; wings have a beautiful lacy pattern, sometimes extending onto the pronotum; pronotum extends back a short distance onto the abdomen; pronotum is often extended sideways and forward over the head to form a type of hood

Habits Mainly found sitting around on the leaves of their food plant or plants; in some species nymphs often remain together to form quite large groups

Breeding Females insert eggs into leaves of food plants; a number of species show maternal care of their offspring

Diet All species feed on plants; some on just one species, others on a range of different species

Habitat Meadows, grassland, woodland, and deserts; wherever their food plants are found

Distribution Worldwide, but fewer in number in colder areas

⤒ *The lace bug* Stephanitis pyri *is found all over the world. It shows the delicate, lacelike wing pattern that is typical of the family. Length 0.1–0.15 inches (3–4 mm).*

Lace Bugs
Tingidae

Without a powerful hand lens or a microscope it is impossible to appreciate the true beauty of some members of the family Tingidae.

THE COMMON NAME OF LACE BUG accurately describes the amazing netlike patterns seen on some species—even though they may be invisible to the naked eye. All known members of the family Tingidae feed on plants. Some can cause considerable damage to forest trees. For example, *Corythuca arcuata*, the oak lace bug from North America, affects the growth of oak trees by damaging large areas of leaves as it feeds. *Stephanitis rhododendri* is a pest of rhododendrons but only where the plants themselves are not a pest. As in some aphids, a few lace bugs cause galls to form on their host plant. The female lays eggs into the plant tissue, which becomes irritated and grows abnormally around the eggs, forming a gall. The young bugs hatch out and feed on the cells in the gall.

Some lace bugs feed on mosses. While a few individuals in each moss-feeding species have full-sized wings, most have short wings, and the pronotum is noticeably flattened, possibly to help them move around easily among the closely packed moss plants. The female spear thistle lace bug, *Tingis cardui* from Europe, lays her eggs carefully on the leaves of the food plant, avoiding the dense felt of fine hairs on the underside of the leaves that would trap the newly hatched nymphs as they make their way to the stem and the flower head.

Different Appearances
It is hard to believe that adult lace bugs and nymphs are from the same species. The adults are normally pale brown, sometimes with darker markings, and often covered in wax. The nymphs, however, are very dark and lack the lace patterns of the adult. Instead, they are covered with spines.

⤷ *Adult creeping thistle lace bugs,* Tingis ampliata, *take sap from a flower bud of their host plant,* Cirsium arvense, *in an English meadow.*

Eggplant Lace Bug

The eggplant lace bug, *Gargaphia solani,* can be found living out its existence on various species of *Solanum* plants (including horse nettle) in North America and Mexico. Like many bees and wasps, the bug is "subsocial," meaning that the female looks after her eggs and then cares for her offspring until they become adult.

The little bugs can produce hordes of young each year. In Maryland, for example, they have been known to have as many as seven generations annually. Each female lays around 100 eggs, taking three to four days to complete the job. The eggs are stuck to the underside of a host plant leaf to form a tight mass. Once the egg laying is complete, the female stops being a layer and takes on the role of carer. She remains with the eggs for roughly six days—the time it takes for them to reach the hatching stage. She then stays with the nymphs until they become adult.

While she is caring for them, the female will actively defend her young. Should a potentially dangerous insect approach the nymphs, she will rush at it with her wings raised and, if necessary, prod it with her head. Experiments where females were removed from their

A large mass of dark-colored late instar nymphs of the eggplant lace bug, Gargaphia solani. *The paler bugs with them are either females on guard or newly emerged adults, or a mixture of the two.*

protecting role showed a considerable reduction in the number of offspring that survived to become adult.

One interesting twist to the story is that some females do not bother to look after their eggs and young themselves. Instead, they let another female do it by laying their eggs in her nest. These so-called "egg dumpers" gain quite an advantage from their apparently careless act: Not only does another bug do all the dangerous work of protecting the eggs, but the first female can continue laying further batches of eggs in the nests of other females. She thereby increases the total number of eggs laid and—with luck—the total number of her offspring that survive.

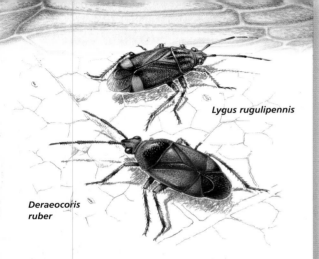

Lygus rugulipennis

Deraeocoris ruber

Common name Plant bugs (leaf bugs, capsid bugs)

Family Miridae

Suborder Heteroptera

Order Hemiptera

Number of species About 10,000 (about 1,800 U.S.)

Size From about 0.12 in (3 mm) to 0.6 in (15 mm)

Key features Shape variable; some long and thin, others short, broad, and rather soft bodied; usually fully winged but may have short wings or lack them altogether; often brightly colored, but many species also have cryptic coloration, usually rather shiny; separated from other bug families by having a 4-segmented rostrum, 4-segmented antennae, and by absence of ocelli

Habits Most often found running around on the plant species with which they are associated

Breeding Females insert eggs into the tissues of their food plants or beneath bark

Diet Many species feed on plants and include pests of crops; others are predaceous, feeding on small insects; some species rob spiders' webs

Habitat Found from the ground up to the tops of the highest trees in almost any habitat where suitable plants grow

Distribution Worldwide

⤒ **Lygus rugulipennis** *is a pest of greenhouse cucumber crops. Length approximately 0.2 inches (5–6 mm).* **Deraeocoris ruber** *feeds on the developing fruit and seeds of numerous plants, as well as on aphids and other small insects. Length 0.2–0.3 inches (6–8 mm). Both species are widespread in the Northern Hemisphere.*

Plant Bugs

Miridae

The Miridae is the second largest family in the Hemiptera, exceeded in numbers of species only by the leafhoppers. A random sweep with a net through any vegetation will almost certainly catch one or more species of plant bugs.

WITH SUCH A LARGE NUMBER of species in the family there is some variation in structure among its members. Typical members are fully winged with oval to elongate bodies when viewed from above. Some species, however, have wings that are reduced in size or completely absent, while others have individuals with full or partial wings. Other species may have fully winged males and wingless females. Coloring ranges from camouflage browns and greens to bright reds and yellows, often with black markings.

Walking on Leaves

The success of the family, with its thousands of species, can be explained partly by the ability to walk easily on any kind of leaf, even the shiniest ones. That is because in adults the tarsi (the "feet") have modifications—varying from one subfamily to another—that help them stick to the surface on which they are walking. Nymphs have an even more interesting way of holding on in an emergency: They push the rectum, the end part of the intestine, out of the tip of the abdomen. The rectum sticks hard to the surface on which they are standing, preventing them from falling or being pulled off. When the emergency is over, they pull the rectum back in again and continue about their business.

In the Miridae the second segment of the legs, the trochanter, is rather unusual. It appears to be made up of two sections, a feature not found in any other bugs, but occurring in spiders. The point where the segment is apparently separated into two is in fact a line of weakness. If a predator grabs a bug by the leg, the trochanter breaks in two, and the bug escapes on its remaining legs. The predator is

⊘ *Adults of the common green capsid bug,* Lygocoris pabulinus, *feed on flowers of charlock,* Sinapis arvensis, *a member of the cabbage family. This common and widespread European bug can be a pest at times, especially on fruit bushes and trees.*

left with just a leg, which is of no particular use since it contains little in the way of food.

Ant mimicry is not uncommon in the family. In some species the nymphs resemble the ant; in others it is the adults. Some bugs are shaped like ants, while others are colored in such a way that they look like ants at first glance and will easily fool a predator, if not an observant human. Among four aphid-feeding *Pilophorus* species, all of which mimic ants, the aphids that they feed on are tended by ants. By mimicking them, the bug escapes the attentions of predators, which keep away from the biting ants. The ants, however, are not fooled by the deception, so the bugs have to be both observant and agile to prevent themselves from being attacked.

In temperate regions there is usually just one generation each year, and overwintering occurs at the egg stage. In the tropics breeding may take place all year round. The female plant bug has a sawlike ovipositor that she uses to cut a slit into plant tissue where she lays her eggs—up to 200 during her lifetime.

Diverse Feeders

Although the common name for the whole family is plant bugs, they are by no means all plant feeders. For example, the members of the subfamily Deraeocorinae are all predators. They feed on small insects, their larvae, mites, and

⊕ *The European bug,* Miris striatus, *is one of the larger species in the family Miridae. It lives on a range of tree species and preys on aphids, scale insects, insect eggs, and small moth larvae.*

other small arthropods, although they will occasionally probe plant material. *Stethoconus* species in the family specialize in preying on lace bugs. *Stephanitis pyrioides*, the azalea lace bug, was accidentally introduced into North America, where it has become a pest on cultivated azaleas. Fortunately, its main predator, *Stethoconus japonicus*, has now been deliberately introduced. It is hoped that it will help control the pest lace bug.

Among the plant-feeding mirids there are those that use just one or a few species of plant, while others are generalists and can feed on almost anything. One subfamily, the Bryocorinae, specializes in ferns or orchids, although *Sahlbergella singularis* is a major pest on cocoa plants. The group is mainly tropical in distribution, but it is also represented in North America and Europe by a number of species that feed on ferns. The small, shiny brown bugs are in fact among the few creatures that actually feed on ferns, which tend to be rather distasteful. Yet another subfamily, the grass

⊕ A large group of tiny
Pachypoda guatemalensis
on the flower of an
Anthurium in rain forest
in Costa Rica. Mirids are
generally not common in
tropical rain forests.

bugs (Mirinae), is confined to feeding on the leaves, flowers, and seeds of grasses, sedges, and rushes at all stages of the life cycle. The adults are often very difficult to pick out since they are pale green to yellowish in color and often resemble grass seeds. They can occur in very large numbers in grassland. The European grass-feeding meadow plant bug, *Leptoterna dolobrata*, has been accidentally introduced into North America, where it is something of a pest.

Pest and Pest Controller

Plant bugs feed by pushing the rostrum into the plant tissue and injecting saliva into the wound, leaving damage marks on the plant. As a consequence, a number of plant bugs are considered pests of human crops. One such species is the tarnished plant bug, *Lygus lineolaris*, from North America. The problem is

that it will feed on almost anything, making it a pest of both crops and forestry. For example, it feeds on young pine trees growing in nurseries, damaging the growing point and making the plants useless. It also likes strawberries: It eats the seeds on the fruit surface, damaging the surrounding flesh and making the fruit unfit for human consumption. In the warm south the bug can have up to five generations each year, so the problem can be very serious.

At the other end of the scale are plant bugs that benefit humans. One example is *Tytthus mundulus*, an Australian species that was introduced into Hawaii early in the 20th century to control the sugarcane leafhopper, *Perkinsiella saccharicida*—itself an introduction from Australia. The leafhopper is now found on sugarcane in Florida, but it seems to cause little damage to the crop there.

⊕ All members of the
subfamily Deraeocorinae
are believed to be
predaceous. An adult
Deraeocoris ruber feeds
on a newly emerged
seven-spot ladybug,
Coccinella 7-punctata, by
the side of an English
meadow.

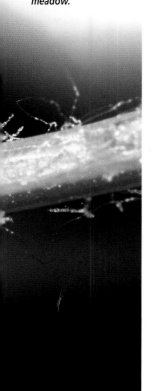

Living with Spiders

Strange as it may seem, *Ranzovius* species mirid bugs have become dependent on a number of different species of spiders and live alongside them in their webs. The bugs spend the whole of their life cycle in the presence of the spiders, relying on them for shelter and for a supply of food. These so-called spider bugs are only found in the New World, with three species in North America.

A good example of a bug successfully living with spiders is *Ranzovius contubernalis* from eastern North America. The bug has been found living with both *Anelosimus studiosus*, a comb-footed spider, and *Agelenopsis pennsylvanica*, a sheet-web weaving spider. During the day both bug adults and nymphs can be found on the spiders' webs or on vegetation close to them. They seem to be less active at night, possibly because that is when the spiders are most active. Webs of both spider species contain a platform consisting of a sheet of silk, and the bug is able to walk both above and beneath the sheet without getting stuck. As the bugs move around on the web, their antennae are in constant motion, but their movements appear not to be noticed by the resident spider. It seems that the small size of the bugs and the vibrations they make in the web are totally unlike those of an insect that has fallen in and is struggling to escape, so the spider ignores them.

The bugs mainly feed on insects trapped in the web that are too small for the spider to bother with. Adults have also been seen to feed on larger insects from which the spider hosts have already fed. It would seem that the dried corpses still contain enough food to interest the bugs. The bugs also feed on any suitable plant material that falls into the web. *Ranzovius contubernalis* occasionally betrays its host spider: It has been seen feeding on the newly molted baby spiderlings belonging to *Anelosimus studiosus*.

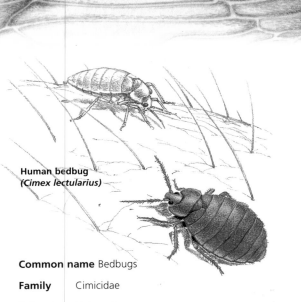

Human bedbug
(*Cimex lectularius*)

Common name	Bedbugs
Family	Cimicidae
Suborder	Heteroptera
Order	Hemiptera
Number of species	About 80 (4 U.S.)
Size	From about 0.1 in (3 mm) to 0.2 in (5 mm)
Key features	Body oval and flattened (appearing more rounded after a blood feed); color yellowish to brown; wingless
Habits	All species are parasites on surface of birds and mammals, including humans; active by night, when they come out to feed
Breeding	Male bugs penetrate the body of the female and inject sperm into the body fluid; eggs are laid in crevices near the host animal
Diet	Blood feeders
Habitat	Birds' nests, cellars, and caves inhabited by bats; human habitations
Distribution	Worldwide, but mostly in the tropics

⊕ *The human bedbug,* Cimex lectularius, *is a notorious worldwide pest. It feeds not only on humans but also on bats, chickens, and other domestic animals. When feeding, it moves slowly over the skin, biting every few steps. It can survive for over a year without a blood meal. Length 0.2–0.3 inches (4–7 mm).*

Bedbugs

Cimicidae

Imagine what it must be like to go to bed knowing that when the light goes off, a host of tiny blood-sucking bugs will emerge from nooks and crannies in the room. Unfortunately for their host, they are sure to indulge in a blood feast.

IN POORER COUNTRIES the bedbug is extremely common, but in the developed world the bedbug is rare today thanks to improved living standards. However, that was not the case even as recently as the middle of the last century. In London, England, just before World War II (1939–1945) as many as 4 million people had bedbugs in their dwellings.

When they do occur, they can be a problem. One family had to vacate their house after they experienced an infestation of bedbugs after bringing them back in their luggage from Europe.

Sending the Bugs to Sleep

One way to get rid of the bugs, however, is to use sleeping tablets—not on the bugs but on the humans. When the bugs feed on people who have taken the tablets, they also take in the drug and fall asleep, leaving themselves to be discovered and destroyed the next morning. The problem bugs are gone in just a few nights.

There are two species of bedbugs that feed on humans. *Cimex lectularius* is the bedbug found in the temperate regions of the world, while *C. rotundatus* (also called *C. hemipterus*) is the bedbug found in the tropics. Both species are similar in appearance: They have a flattened, rounded body that is dark brown and wingless. There are differences in the behavior

⊖ *Cimex lectularius, the bedbugs of temperate regions, crawls across a bedcover in search of human blood. Its flattened body allows it to squeeze into narrow cracks to hide during daylight hours.*

⊕ *A* Cimex *species bedbug showing the rostrum with which it sucks up its blood meals. From the swollen state of its body it is clear that it has just fed.*

of the two species, which mainly relate to the difference in temperatures where they live. The tropical bedbug is a much faster mover than the temperate species, which means that it is capable of traveling greater distances and spreading more quickly from one place to another.

Virus Spreaders?

Nymph and adult bugs of both species spend the hours of daylight in any suitable nook or cranny, coming out to feed at night. Although their bites are a minor irritation producing itching and swelling, they are not dangerous. Generally bedbugs have not been known to transmit any important human diseases. Recent studies, however, indicate that they may be involved in passing on the hepatitis B virus.

Females attach their eggs to a surface, usually in their resting place. The eggs take between 10 and 20 days to hatch. Female bugs may lay between 150 and 345 eggs during their average life span of nine to 18 months. On hatching, the nymphs must take a blood meal during each of their six instars; otherwise they cannot molt into the next instar.

Flower Bugs

The flower bugs, or minute pirate bugs (their other common name), in the family Anthocoridae are small bugs with a worldwide distribution. They are closely related to the bedbugs and are sometimes included within the family Cimicidae. The flower bugs are usually fully winged, rather flat insects with an oval or oblong shape when viewed from above. The front of the head juts forward like a sort of snout. While a few of them feed on blood, including that of humans, most of them eat other insects and mites.

They are very careful predators. In fact, biologists call them "timid predators" because they usually only feed on prey that is smaller than themselves and that moves relatively slowly. Their prey includes aphids, thrips, barklice, whiteflies, and mites as well as the eggs and smaller larvae of various insects. As a result, the little flower bugs are quite important in helping control the numbers of some important pests.

One interesting feature of some species is that either by accident, or perhaps by design, they will also attack humans. As its name implies, the European common flower bug, *Anthocoris nemorum*, is common on flowers during the summer months. It flies freely and often lands on bare human skin. At that point it will insert its proboscis into the victim, who will usually brush it away immediately. Whether the bugs attempt to suck blood is not recorded, but the site of the puncture wound usually swells up and can itch for a considerable time.

Field damsel bug
(*Nabis feras*)

Common name Damsel bugs

Family Nabidae

Suborder Heteroptera

Order Hemiptera

Number of species About 300 (48 U.S.)

Size From about 0.16 in (4 mm) to 0.5 in (13 mm)

Key features Body rather long, often more slender in front, the abdomen broadening out behind; normal color range from dirty yellow to dark brown; eyes large; rostrum with 4 segments, long and curved beneath the head; front legs adapted for holding prey; some species wingless, others may have long- or short-winged as well as wingless forms

Habits Fairly active bugs walking around on the ground or on herbs, trees, and bushes in search of prey

Breeding Little or no courtship known; males just jump onto a female and mate; eggs laid in plant stems

Diet Other insects and spiders, and their eggs

Habitat Grassland, forest, damp places, and deserts

Distribution Found in all areas of the world

⊕ The field damsel bug, Nabis feras, *is found across the Northern Hemisphere. Members of the genus* Nabis *are the most abundant damsel bugs found in crops, especially field crops such as alfalfa and soybean. Length approx. 0.3 inches (7–9 mm).*

Damsel Bugs
Nabidae

Their common name implies that damsel bugs are gentle insects, but that is far from the truth. They are in fact killers, sneaking up stealthily on suitable small prey before plunging their long, curved rostrum into them and sucking them dry.

DAMSEL BUGS ARE USUALLY pale yellowish-brown to dark brown, sometimes black. They live on the ground or on vegetation. At first glance they resemble assassin bugs because their front legs are adapted for holding prey, although they are not as strongly developed as those of the assassin bugs. The other main difference between the two is that the rostrum of assassin bugs is short, thick, and has three segments, while that of damsel bugs is longer, curved, slim, and with four segments.

Although the lifestyles of the bugs from the two families are similar, the damsel bugs are more closely related to the bedbugs and flower bugs (Anthocoridae) than to the assassin bugs. Lack of wings, or at least the inability to fly, is quite common in the family Nabidae. That may be because they walk long distances in search of prey and therefore do not need to fly in order to reach new habitats.

Insect Eaters
Damsel bugs feed on a wide range of other arthropods, including aphids, caterpillars, beetle larvae, leafhoppers, and other plant bugs. Moth and beetle eggs are also eaten. All stages of the life cycle are predators, and it appears that they detect their prey both by its scent and by observing its movements.

In a small way damsel bugs are important in keeping down the numbers of arthropod pests. For example, in North America damsel bugs prey on pests such as the corn earworm, *Heliothis zea*, the European corn borer, *Ostrinia nubilalis*, and the cabbage worm, *Pieris rapae*.

↗ *An adult marsh damsel bug, Dolichonabis limbatus, a European species, feeds on the nymph of a stink bug. The bug seems unaffected by the unpleasant secretions produced by the nymph's stink glands.*

→ *These tiny black-and-white insects are Arachnocoris species damsel bugs. They live in spider webs in the Amazonian forests of Brazil.*

They also feed on the eggs and nymphs of the Colorado potato beetle, *Leptinotarsa decimlineata,* and the asparagus beetle, *Crioceris asparagi.* The European tree damsel bug, *Himacerus apterus*, is known to prey on two major pests—the red spider mite and caterpillars of the gypsy moth.

Careless Coupling

Breeding is very straightforward. Males simply grab the nearest seemingly suitable bug, which sometimes turns out to be another male. If the partner is female and receptive, they mate. The way in which the sperm gets to the eggs to fertilize them links the family Nabidae with the bedbugs (Cimicidae). In the damsel bug subfamily Prostemminae the sperm passes into the female's blood and makes its way to the ovaries, just as it does in the bedbugs. In the subfamily Nabinae, however, it takes the more usual route along the female's reproductive tubes. The females lay their eggs into the stems of grasses, reeds, and other plants.

The early instar nymphs of some species are very good ant mimics, which gives them some protection from the attentions of their enemies. The European damsel bug, *Himacerus mirmicoides*, for example, has young nymphs that resemble the black ant, *Lasius niger*. The resemblance to the ant is so strong that they even have similar spines on the thorax and abdomen, and a slim waist just like the ant's. The waist is not real, however, but "painted on." The outer edges of the first and second abdominal segment are white, leaving a slim black line down the center that represents the bug's nonexistent waist.

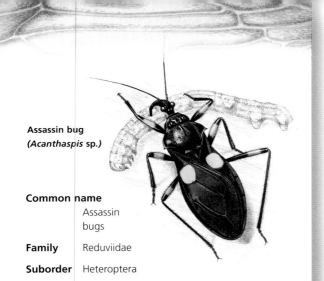

Assassin bug
(*Acanthaspis* sp.)

Common name
Assassin bugs

Family Reduviidae

Suborder Heteroptera

Order Hemiptera

Number of species About 5,000 (106 U.S.)

Size From about 0.3 in (8 mm) to 1.6 in (4 cm)

Key features General shape oval to elongate, some actually resembling small stick insects; short, stout, curved, 3-segmented rostrum that fits in a groove beneath the thorax when not in use; noticeable groove across head behind the eyes; front legs adapted for clasping prey, so they usually walk on the hind 2 pairs; pronotum may have a crest or may bear spikes, which may also occur on top of the head

Habits Walk around on vegetation and on the ground in search of prey, often moving slowly and stealthily; blood-sucking species find their prey by flying in search of it; some species attract prey by using "tools" such as resin

Breeding Females of a number of species exhibit parental care, as do males in some species

Diet Other insects and their larvae; spiders; the blood of vertebrates; one species known to feed on liquid from fermenting dung

Habitat Many species live on vegetation, while others live on the ground or on tree bark; some species inhabit the nests of termites; found in all kinds of habitat—grassland, forests, marshes, and deserts

Distribution Worldwide, but with the greatest variety of species in the tropical regions

⊕ *An* Acanthaspis *species assassin bug feeds on a caterpillar.* Acanthaspis *species have been found in West Africa, where they prey on ants. They camouflage themselves by attaching the sucked-out bodies of ants to their back by means of fine hairs and silk threads. Length 1 inch (2.5 cm).*

Assassin Bugs
Reduviidae

The Reduviidae are a bit like "hit men": quiet assassins that kill without remorse. Not only that, they are such efficient killers that they can take on prey considerably larger than themselves.

THE LARGE, MAINLY TROPICAL family Reduviidae varies considerably in body form, from heavily built to delicate and gnatlike, and from short and broad to long and thin. However, they all have common features that separate them from other bug families. Their three-segmented rostrum is a fearsome piece of equipment: short, broad, and used for stabbing through a weak part of the prey's exoskeleton. At the same time, the victim is held in the powerful front pair of legs. Saliva is then injected, which rapidly paralyzes the prey and then digests its internal organs, leaving behind a "soup" for the bug to suck up. As with other predaceous

⊕ *A closeup of the head of* Canthesancus gulo *from Sumatra reveals the robust, curved mouthparts with which it stabs and then feeds from its victims.*

① A warningly colored assassin bug, Eulyes amaena *from Malaysia. Its overall shape is representative of what might be termed "the typical assassin bug."*

① It is hard to believe that an assassin bug nymph from Kenya is hidden here. It is camouflaged beneath bits of wood, soil, and the empty husks of its victims.

bugs, larger members of the family should be approached with care, since if picked up they can bite very painfully. The rostrum also has a second use as a stridulatory organ. In nearly all male assassin bugs the tip can be rubbed against a sort of file on the underside of the thorax to produce sounds. In some species that can be heard as a distinct squeak and is probably a warning to "keep off." Otherwise the sounds are produced to attract females.

Clever Assassins

While many species of assassin bug sit quietly until a suitable victim comes within reach or steal slowly around until they find a victim, others have developed more cunning ways of ensuring that they find a meal. One way is to live among their victims, but making sure they are not recognized. In Central America both adults and nymphs of the bug *Salyavata variegata* are found in the nests of *Nasutitermes* species termites. The adult bugs have camouflage coloring, while the nymphs disguise themselves by scraping off pieces of the termite nest surface and gluing them to their bodies. The bugs sit by the termite nest openings,

⬆ **Apiomeris flaviventris,** *an assassin bug from Mexico, is busy feeding on a small bee that it has captured in its desert habitat.*

grabbing suitable-sized victims as they emerge. The third, fourth, and fifth instar nymphs go one step farther, using the sucked-dry body of one of their victims as a "tool" to attract more termites to their doom.

A Sticky Death

"Tools" are used by other assassin bugs to lure and trap prey. In Southeast Asia two species, *Ectinoderus longimanus* and *Amulius malayus*, have been given the common name of resin bugs. They dip their hairy front legs into resin that exudes from various trees. The resin is also used by *Trigona* species stingless bees to build their nests. As a result, they approach the resin-coated bugs, expecting some nest-building material, only to receive an unpleasant and fatal surprise. *Manicoris rufipes* from Brazil also catches stingless bees, but uses a mixture of pollen, nectar, and resin to coat its front legs.

The bug reaches out toward any bee attracted to it. On contact with the sticky legs the bee becomes trapped and ends up as a meal. Also in Brazil *Apiomerus* species assassin bug nymphs have been discovered "fishing" for termites. They attach sticky resin to their front legs, find a hole in the tunnels through which tree-nesting termites run, and sit and wait. As a termite runs past, they touch it on the back, it sticks to their legs, is hauled out of the tunnel, and speared with the rostrum.

Living in the south of the United States is the assassin bug, *Stenolemus lanipes*, which specializes in a creature that is itself a predator—the common American house spider *Achaeranea tepidariorum*. Clearly in order to avoid being eaten by the spider, the bugs have to behave in a very clever way. As its name indicates, the spider constructs its web on houses or other buildings, and the young spiders remain in the web with their mother for some weeks before eventually going their own way. It is the youngsters that the bug targets. On the bug's legs are tiny spines that become covered with either spider silk or some other silklike material, which acts to camouflage it and allows it to walk on the spider's web without getting stuck. The bug first steals up to the web and taps on it with its antennae. It then walks onto the web, vibrating its body, which

Bloodsuckers

All species within one subfamily of assassin bugs, the Triatominae, suck the blood of vertebrate animals, including humans. Such attacks are always painful and unpleasant experiences; however, in Central and South America the situation can be dangerous, since the bugs carry the infective organisms of Chaga's disease. The disease itself is caused by a single-celled animal, or protozoan, related to the organisms that cause sleeping sickness in Africa. Although it occasionally kills children early on in the infection, the disease does not normally produce any symptoms until 10 to 20 years after being bitten by the bug. The main effect of the disease is to damage the heart. People who contract it, mainly poor country folk, can expect to live on average nine years fewer than an uninfected person. It is believed that between 16 and 18 million people have the disease at any one time. However, only around 50,000 die as a result each year, making it nothing like as dangerous as malaria, another killer disease transmitted by insects.

Infection can occur through bites, but may also result if the bug's droppings are rubbed into an open scratch or other wound, or into the eye. Infection can also occur if food contaminated with the bug's droppings is eaten. One of the bugs that carries the disease, *Triatoma sanguisuga*, the eastern blood-sucking cone-nose, is found from Ontario down to Florida and across as far as Texas. Although it carries Chaga's disease farther south into southern Mexico, it does not carry it any farther north. While the bug is quite capable of flying to find a host when it is hungry, after a blood feed it is so heavy that it is unable to leave the ground.

⤒ *The bloodsucking cone-nose,* Triatoma sanguisuga, *is also called the Mexican bedbug. Its bites are hardly felt by its hosts, but the results can be fatal.*

This unusual bug lives both as nymph and adult in crevices under stones close to nests of the ant *Anoplolepis longipes* and nowhere else. No ants, no bugs! At night bugs of all ages emerge from their daytime hiding places and, accompanied by the ants, make their way to where they feed on masses of fermenting cow dung. The bugs feed on the liquid oozing from it. The dung has to be at just the right stage of fermentation to be of use to the bugs, which may have to travel some distance to find such a food source. As a result, groups of bugs living around a number of different ant nests may all end up at the same feeding place, returning to their own particular nest during the day. The ants appear to feed on the bugs' droppings.

Caring Parents

Some Reduviidae species indulge in parental care, but it is not common. Females of *Rhinocoris carmelita* and *Pisilus tipuliformis*, both from Africa, stand guard on or near their eggs until they hatch. *Ghilianella* species from South America do a bit more—the female carries her small brood around with her, the infants maintaining contact by wrapping their long, slim legs around her body.

Paternal care is very rare among insects, but occurs in some *Rhinocoris* species assassin bugs from Africa. The reason for its rarity is that no male insect can be sure that it was his sperm

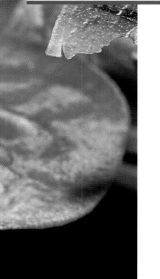

in turn vibrates the web in much the same way as a piece of leaf blown into the web by the wind might do. The movement of the web is ignored by the spider, and the bug is allowed to get within striking distance of a youngster while keeping well away from the adult spider.

Assassin bugs that are not killers are exceptional, but one such species is *Lophocephala guerini* from India and Sri Lanka.

← *Some assassin bugs mimic social or parasitic wasps. The curved rostrum of* Hiranetis braconiformis *from Peru, however, reveals it to be a bug, not a wasp.*

Left: A female Pisilus tipuliformis assassin bug stands guard over her newly hatched nymphs in rain forest in Uganda. Below: Rhinocoris tristis *is a species of assassin bug from Kenya whose males stand guard over the eggs laid by their mates. The main job of the male is to prevent tiny parasitic wasps from laying their own eggs in the eggs that belong to him.*

that fertilized the eggs. Caring for eggs fertilized by another male would be a waste of time. *Rhinocoris albopilosus* has overcome the problem: Having found a receptive female, he mates with her several times and then stays with or very close to her while she lays her eggs. As soon as she has finished, he quickly moves in and sits over the egg batch, remaining there whatever the circumstances, foregoing any food unless some unwitting insect ventures too close.

While he is on guard, he is regularly visited by the female, with whom he again mates. She then adds more eggs to the batch he is guarding. The male gains a further advantage from his behavior: His presence at a batch of eggs is very attractive to other females that are looking for a male to protect their eggs. As long as they first allow him to mate with them (so that he is certain that he is the one that has fertilized their eggs), they are allowed to add to the batch that he is protecting. He stays with the eggs until all of the nymphs have emerged, when he abandons them. His natural predatory instincts are switched off in some way at this particular time, since he does not attempt to spear and feed on any of his offspring.

Why do the males protect their eggs? There are certainly insects around that feed on eggs, and the male will drive them off. However, the greatest enemies are tiny parasitic wasps that lay their eggs into the bug eggs in order for their larvae to feed on the developing

nymph. *Rhinocoris* males have been observed darting at the female wasps, attempting to spear them on their rostrum. The presence of such attentive males certainly increases the survival rate of the offspring, but not all of the wasps are driven away; out of a number of the eggs a tiny wasp, rather than a bug, will eventually emerge.

The males of some *Zelus* species assassin bugs from Colombia are even more caring. They guard the egg batches until they hatch, but then they stay with the nymphs. They are attentive fathers, catching prey and holding it at the end of their stretched-out rostrum. The nymphs all cluster around and feed from the prey. The male's efforts are rewarded: Studies have shown that in unprotected egg batches 55 percent of eggs were found to be parasitized by wasps, compared with only 21 percent of eggs that were guarded.

Some larger assassin bugs, such as this Arilus *species from Peru, called a "wheel bug," are quite prepared to go into an attack posture if they feel threatened.*

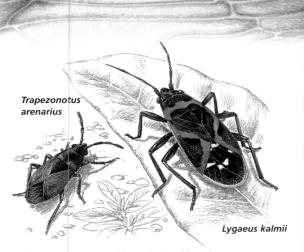

Trapezonotus arenarius

Lygaeus kalmii

Common name Seed bugs (ground bugs)

Family Lygaeidae

Suborder Heteroptera

Order Hemiptera

Number of species About 3,000 (295 U.S.)

Size From about 0.09 in (2.2 mm) to 0.8 in (20 mm)

Key features Rather tough-bodied bugs, mostly oval in shape; some longer and thinner species; body usually appears flat topped; ocelli present; fully and partially winged as well as wingless forms and species; front femurs enlarged in many species; most are combinations of black and brown; a few are brightly colored

Habits Found either on the plant that produces seeds on which they feed or running around on the ground beneath

Breeding Sound production is involved in courtship in many seed bugs; eggs usually laid on or into food plants

Diet The vast majority are seed feeders; others specialize in insect eggs and larvae; a few are blood suckers

Habitat Forests, grasslands, meadows, gardens, marshes, seashore, and deserts

Distribution Worldwide

⤒ *The small eastern milkweed bug,* Lygaeus kalmii *from the United States, feeds and lays its eggs on milkweed plants. The bug is immune to the toxic chemicals in milkweed but is itself toxic to other insect predators. Length 0.4–0.5 inches (10–13 mm).* Trapezonotus arenarius *is a less common species from the Northern Hemisphere, where it lives on savanna. Length 0.15–0.2 inches (4–5 mm).*

Seed Bugs

Lygaeidae

Seed bugs is an appropriate common name for the Lygaeidae, since the majority feed on seeds of a range of plant species, including trees. They are also called ground bugs because they feed on seeds that have fallen from the plant onto the ground.

SEED BUGS ARE AMONG the drabbest-colored bugs, with most being shades of brown to black. There are, however, notable exceptions such as the warningly colored, distasteful large milkweed bugs of the genus *Oncopeltus,* which have black-and-orange patterning.

While most seed bugs live away from the coast, a few species are found on the seashore, including salt marshes. *Henestaris* species from Europe and Asia live in such habitats, as well as inland alongside salt pans. *Henestaris halophilus* is widespread in the region and is also found in a few salt marshes, where it feeds on the seeds of sea purslane, *Atriplex portulacoides.* As the tide comes in, the nymphs remain submerged on the food plant without coming to harm.

Saliva Injection

Seed-feeding Lygaeidae inject saliva into the seed to digest it before sucking up the liquid that results. Those that do not feed on seeds but on the plants themselves puncture single or groups of plant cells and suck the sap out of them. With around 3,000 species in the family a number have become pests by attacking the seed crops on which humans depend.

Perhaps the most important seed bug pests in North America are the chinch bugs of the genus *Blissus. Blissus leucopterus,* a very widespread species, is a particular problem. The adults overwinter in bunches of wild grasses, but on emerging in spring they then move into fields of cultivated crops such as wheat, barley, and other small-grained cereals. As these ripen and dry out, further generations of the bug move onto crops such as corn and

⤒ *A mating pair of* Neacoryphus bicrucis *on ragweed flowers in the Great Smoky Mountains of Tennessee. Like a number of seed bugs, this species wears a red-and-black "warning" uniform.*

Large Femora

It is not unusual in seed bugs for the front femora to be enlarged and to bear teeth or spines. It was first thought that they were used to help hold seeds while the bugs were feeding. Research into the courtship of a European seed bug, *Scolopostethus affinis*, has indicated that the development of the femora may be for a different purpose altogether. Both males and females of the bug use their femora aggressively during courtship. Since males are usually more aggressive during such activities, they would be expected to have bigger femora in relation to their size. That is indeed the case, so perhaps they are not enlarged for seed holding.

sorghum. The damage caused is the result of feeding from sap at the base of the young plants, which show poor growth as a result.

The bugs have an unpleasant smell, which may explain why they have few natural enemies. Another species of chinch bug, *Blissus occidus*, is a pest on buffalo grass, *Buchloc dactyloides,* while *Blissus insularis*, the southern chinch bug, attacks St. Augustine grass, *Stenotaphrum secundatum*, which is grown as a turf and pasture grass.

In parts of Europe *Lygaeus equestris* is a problem bug because it feeds on the seeds of the sunflower, which is a very important crop plant. Although the bugs probe only the seeds in the outer rings on the sunflower seed heads, nevertheless the damage they cause can result in as much as a 2 percent drop in production.

Helpful Bugs

Among the few predaceous seed bugs are a few species that are known to be of help in controlling other insects that are pests—most notably the big-eyed bug, *Geocoris punctipes,* in North America. The bug feeds on a whole range of small insects, but it lives in fields of alfalfa, cotton, and soybean, where it helps control the numbers of pests such as aphids and whiteflies. It is being looked at as a possible biological control insect in greenhouse systems. The closely related big-eyed bug *G. pallens* is a predator on other seed bugs as well as spider mites, cotton bollworm larvae, and various leafhoppers.

One New World seed bug, *Clerada apicicornis,* is known to prey on the assassin bug *Rhodnius prolixus. Rhodnius prolixus* lives alongside humans, especially in the country, and carries the rather unpleasant Chaga's disease. Research workers have looked at the possibility that the seed bug might be used to control numbers of the assassin bug, but results have not been encouraging.

Clerada apicicornis is unusual in that it actually requires mammalian blood. It gets it either directly from humans or other animals, or indirectly by taking it from an *R. prolixus* that has already fed from a mammal. That means that, in theory, *C. apicicornis* could also be a transmitter of Chaga's disease. That is unlikely, since given the choice, it prefers secondhand blood from an assassin bug rather than fresh.

Courtship Strategies

Many males of the Lygaeidae stridulate to attract females. Sound is produced by rubbing teeth on the underside of the hind wing against the upper surface of the abdomen. Pheromones are also involved in attracting the opposite sex.

The nettle ground bug, *Heterogaster urticae* from Europe, lives on and under stinging nettles, *Urtica dioica.* They overwinter as adults, often in human habitations. Males and females can gather in very large numbers in some years, so that the nettles appear to be alive with mating pairs. Mating can be very prolonged in the species, the two sexes remaining coupled together for up to four days at a time.

Having gotten together, courtship may be quite involved. Males of the North American ground bug, *Ligyrocoris diffusus,* indulge in a sort of courtship dance. The male moves his body to and fro and regularly pushes his abdomen downward as he stridulates. His

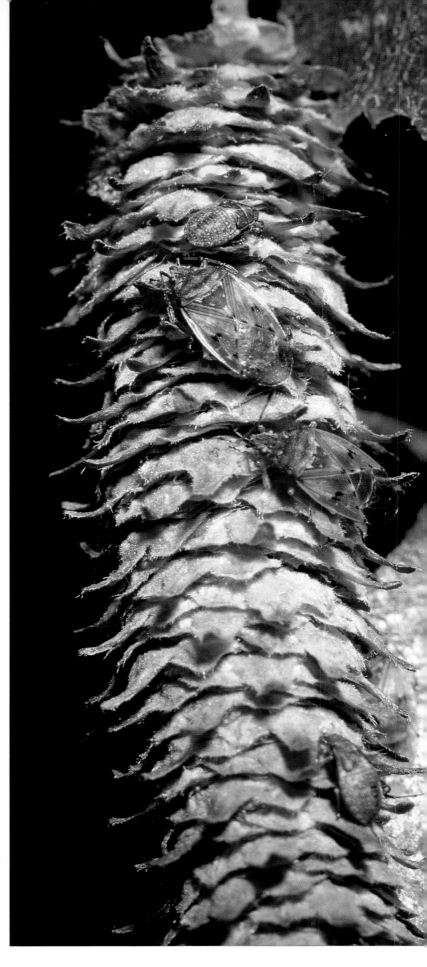

⑦ *A group of warningly colored seed bug nymphs makes a conspicuous sight on a leaf in a rain forest in Kenya. They are clustered together for protection.*

⑥ *Adults and nymphs of the seed bug* Kleidocerys resedae *feeding on developing seeds on a birch tree. The bug occurs in both North America and Europe.*

behavior is probably more to do with telling the females that he is of their species rather than wooing them directly.

Can't Let Go

Having found a mate, it is in the male's interest to hang onto her as long as he can so that other males do not get a chance to mate with her. To prevent that from happening, some male seed bugs indulge in prolonged mating. Mating in the pretty European seed bug *Lygaeus equestris* can last for anything from half an hour to a whole 24 hours. Tellingly, there is no difference in the amount of sperm passed into the female whether copulation is short or long. The idea that males "keep" females is also supported by the fact that when there are fewer males around, mating tends to be brief, but with larger numbers of males the matings last longer.

In the North American ragwort seed bug, *Neacoryphus bicrucis*, the females mate with different males, but it is the last male to mate

that fathers most of the offspring. Once again, the males hang onto the females as long as possible after they have mated.

Courtship in the ragwort seed bug can be hectic if not utterly confused. It occupies the ragwort plants in the company of the leaf-footed bug *Margus obscurator*. The males of both species of bug have been seen chasing and wrestling with females of their own species that have rebuffed their amorous advances and invitations to mate. Sometimes the males are lucky enough to couple with the female when they are in the middle of such a tussle. Things do go wrong, however, and males have been seen chasing and attempting to mate with males of their own species, as well as males and females of other species.

An unusual piece of reproductive behavior has been noted in a New World seed bug, *Oncopeltus baranowskii,* that feeds on fig seeds. While they are mating, the female taps the male gently with her hind legs. It seems that she is testing how good a mate the male is, since the more she taps, the shorter time they mate, and the less likelihood that she will receive a spermatophore.

A Present for the Lady

Another successful way of getting a female to be more inclined to mate is for the male to offer her a sweetener in the form of a nuptial gift. The male of the seed bug *Stilbocoris natalensis* from Africa does so by first finding a suitable fig seed and spearing it on the end of his rostrum. He then injects it with saliva, which digests the seed's contents, before then presenting it to a female. Any female treated so handsomely then allows him to mate with her while she is feeding on his gift; males who come without a gift are simply rejected. One extra advantage to the male of offering the gift is that the food it provides for the female will help form the eggs, which will be fertilized by his sperm and produce his offspring.

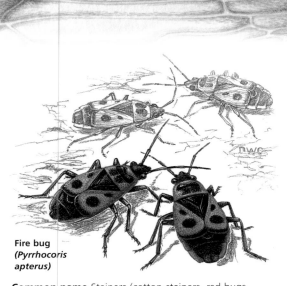

Fire bug
(*Pyrrhocoris apterus*)

Common name Stainers (cotton-stainers, red bugs, fire bugs)

Family Pyrrhocoridae

Suborder Heteroptera

Order Hemiptera

Number of species About 300 (7 U.S)

Size From about 0.3 in (8 mm) to 0.7 in (18 mm)

Key features Resemble seed bugs, but do not have ocelli on the head, and front femurs are never enlarged; also less solidly built than seed bugs and usually brightly colored, often in red and black

Habits Often form large, colorful aggregations on the plants on whose seeds they feed

Breeding Adults produce pheromones to attract one another so that mating can take place; eggs laid on food plants

Diet Nearly all species feed on seeds, fruits, or suck sap from their host plants; a few feed on other insects

Habitat Forests, grassland, deserts, seashore—wherever their particular food plants grow

Distribution Most species are found in warmer climates, mainly in the Old World, with just a few in temperate areas

⊕ Pyrrhocoris apterus, *commonly known as the fire bug, is found throughout the Northern Hemisphere. It displays the red-and-black coloration that is typical of the family. Large groups can be seen feeding on plants in the spring. Length 0.3–0.4 inches (8–12 mm).*

TRUE BUGS

Stainers   Pyrrhocoridae

Since the main colors of members of the family are red and black, and because adults and nymphs are often found together in large groups, stainers are easy to spot.

THE BRIGHT-RED COLORATION of stainers gives them one of their alternative common names of "fire bugs." They use their long, slim proboscis for feeding on seeds. It is on the seed heads of their food plants—most commonly members of the mallow family, Malvaceae—that they are most likely to be found.

Damage by Staining

The name cotton-stainers comes from the bugs' habit of staining cotton (*Gossypium* species) and kapok (*Ceiba pentandra*), two important crops. The main culprits are the *Dysdercus* species "cotton-stainers," found all over the warmer parts of the world. The bugs damage the cotton and kapok fibers as they penetrate the seed case to get to the seeds. As they feed, the seeds leak sap, which stains the fibers. To add to the damage, fungi then feed on the sap.

Sometimes certain species will turn their attention to other crops. In Australia, for example, *Dysdercus sidae*, which normally feeds on native seeds and is a minor pest on cotton, can feed on and damage ripening peaches. Another Australian member of the family, *Dindymus versicolor*, feeds on a wide variety of plants, including important crops such as cotton, apples, pears, plums, grapes, strawberries, and a range of vegetables. In large numbers it can stunt the growth of the plants and also damage the fruit.

Within this mainly sap-feeding family are a few predaceous species. *Antilochus coqueberti* from Japan specializes in feeding on other stainers, including *Dysdercus* species. As a result, it has been investigated for possible use in controlling pests.

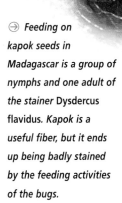

⊖ *Feeding on kapok seeds in Madagascar is a group of nymphs and one adult of the stainer Dysdercus flavidus. Kapok is a useful fiber, but it ends up being badly stained by the feeding activities of the bugs.*

Stilt Bugs

In common with the stainers, the stilt bugs in the family Berytidae may often be found together in very large numbers on their food plants. Stilt bugs have a number of distinctive features that make them instantly recognizable. Their general shape is like that of gnats or small crane flies, with a slim body and long, slim legs. The bugs differ from these other insects in that they have long antennae, the ends of which are distinctly swollen so that they are club shaped. The ends of the tibiae are also enlarged, giving the appearance of swollen knees.

Stilt bugs are close relations of the seed bugs, although they do not look much like them. As in seed bugs, the majority are plant feeders, although the stilt bugs tend to probe the growing parts of the plant rather than seeds. On the other hand, a number of species are predaceous, feeding on aphids or insect eggs.

Although there are only around 180 species worldwide, with 14 species in North America, they are nevertheless a fairly important group for two different

A large group of Parajalysus nigrescens stilt bugs gathers on a plant in rain forest in Peru. When they occur in large numbers, some species can cause damage to cultivated plants.

reasons. First, some stilt bugs are serious crop pests. The spined stilt bug, *Jalysus wickhami*, for example, causes serious damage in North America, especially to tomatoes. *Metacanthus pulchellus* is a pest of bottle gourds and other members of the cucumber family in India.

However, there are other stilt bugs that benefit people by helping control pest insects. In Japan, for example, there is a stilt bug that feeds on soybean aphids, while in Peru a different species attacks cotton aphids and the eggs of the cotton fruitworm.

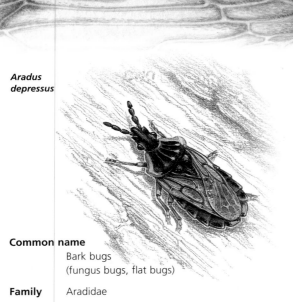

Aradus depressus

Common name
Bark bugs
(fungus bugs, flat bugs)

Family   Aradidae

Suborder   Heteroptera

Order   Hemiptera

Number of species About 1,800 (104 U.S.)

Size   From about 0.12 in (3 mm) to 0.5 in (13 mm)

Key features Body very flattened, usually oval in outline; legs rather short; antennae short and thick; body often covered in small spines or knobs; also may be pitted so that they are rather "toady" in appearance; usually have camouflage coloration of reddish- or dark brown; some species wingless, others may have fully or partially developed wings; maxillae and mandibles long, thin, and coiled up in special chambers inside the head when not in use

Habits   Nearly all live under bark, but a few live on the forest floor in leaf litter or on fungi

Breeding   Male lies below female during mating; maternal (and occasional paternal) care has been noted in the family; in species living in temperate climates there is no particular breeding season; nymphs in colder climates hibernate and develop the following spring

Diet   All are fungus feeders; a few species feed on tree sap

Habitat   Wherever there are trees of a suitable age with loose bark; a number of species recorded among leaf litter in forests

Distribution Worldwide in forested areas

⊕ *Aradus depressus is a European bark bug that lives under the bark of dead trees, where there is a plentiful supply of fungus to feed on. Most* Aradus *species—the largest genus in the family—are from the Northern Hemisphere. Length 0.2–0.3 inches (5–7 mm).*

Bark Bugs

Aradidae

Bark bugs are so thin it is a wonder that there is room for all of their internal organs to fit inside their flattened body.

BARK BUGS ARE EXCEEDINGLY well adapted for life in the very tight, narrow spaces beneath loose bark on the trees on which they exist. The lack of space for movement accounts for many of their distinguishing features. Long, thin antennae would obviously get in the way in a narrow gap, so instead the antennae are short and rather stout. The legs are also short in relation to the size of the body. While some species of bark bug are wingless, in others the wings may be either partially or fully developed.

Wings may also be different in males and females—an example of polymorphism. In the European bark bug *Aradus cinnamomeus* for example, the females can be partially or fully winged. The males have shortened hind wings, and the ends of the forewings are narrowed down so that they cover little of the hind wings. Since they spend most of their life protected beneath bark, it seems that full protection of the delicate hind wings by the more robust forewings is not necessary.

Fungus Eaters

Most bark bugs feed on fungi, especially those that are bringing about the decomposition of dead parts of standing trees or wholly dead trees. Although generally feeding on fungi that invade the wood beneath the bark, there are species that feed on bracket fungi growing out from the surface of the tree and a few that feed on other types of fungus not associated with trees. Bark bugs have a very special adaptation to allow them to feed. Normally in bugs the mandibles and the maxillae—the structures in the rostrum that pierce and suck— are the same length as the rostrum as a whole. However, although the bark bug's rostrum is very short, its feeding structures are long and thin enough to pierce and suck out the

⊕ *Several mating pairs of* Dysodius lunatus *sit on a rotting fallen tree in a rain forest in Costa Rica. The clusters of tiny mites are hitching a ride and do not suck the bugs' blood.*

contents of the long, thin fungus threads from which it feeds. When not in use, they are coiled up into special chambers inside the bug's head.

One or two bark bugs are not fungus feeders but instead feed on sap from the trees beneath whose bark they live. *Aradus cinnamomeus* is one such bug, and it can reach pest proportions in Europe, where it can cause damage to young trees of various kinds, including pines. In North America *A. kormilevi* and *A. antennalis* also feed on tree sap.

Because they spend their lives out of sight, details of the life cycles of most bark bugs are not known. It is known that in a number of species stridulation takes place to bring the sexes together—the sound is produced by rubbing their legs over projections or grooves on the underside of the abdomen. Unusually for terrestrial bugs, the female sits above the male during mating. There is no particular

breeding season for many North American and European bark bugs—an unusual situation for bugs in temperate climates—perhaps as a result of living in the protected environment beneath tree bark. As a result, eggs, nymphs, and adults can be found at almost any time of the year, but there is a tendency for more reproductive activity in the warmer months. However, in the coldest regions the bugs hibernate as nymphs to continue their development the following spring.

Females of the North American bark bug *Neuroctenus pseudonymus* leave their eggs as soon as they have laid them. Another bug— assumed to be the male that mated with her before she laid—then guards the eggs as they develop. It would appear that this is one of the rare instances in the insect world of paternal (rather than the more common maternal) care.

Narnia inornata

Common name Leaf-footed
bugs (squash bugs, tip-wilter bugs, flag-footed bugs)

Family Coreidae

Suborder Heteroptera

Order Hemiptera

Number of species About 2,000 (120 U.S.)

Size From about 0.2 in (5 mm) to 1.7 in (4.3 cm)

Key features Fairly broad-bodied bugs with the head less than half the width of the pronotum and the fourth antennal segment not curved; membrane of the forewings has many parallel veins running across it; femurs of hind legs often either very swollen or have flattened, leaflike extensions; stink glands present

Habits Usually found on the plant or plants from which they feed

Breeding Males and females may come together as individuals, or they may aggregate in large numbers before mating; eggs laid on host plants

Diet Sap from their host plant or plants

Habitat Forests, grassland, orchards, gardens, deserts, and seashore—wherever their particular food plants grow

Distribution Most species are found in the warmer parts of the world, with just a few occurring in temperate areas

⤒ *Narnia inornata is found in Central America. The fat, extended femora complete with spines can be clearly seen. Length approximately 0.6–0.7 inches (15–18 mm).*

Leaf-Footed Bugs

Coreidae

Some of the larger members of the Coreidae look rather sinister. All of them can behave unpleasantly—when an observer gets too close, the bug may shoot a blast of stinking fluid from its rear end.

THE COREIDAE ALL HAVE a common characteristic—the large number of parallel veins on the membranous section of the forewings. Many species also have hind legs that are developed in some way. In some species the hind femora are very fat and often have dangerous spines on them. In others the tibiae are developed, so that they are flattened toward the end to form a leaflike structure or in a few species what looks more like a flag.

Offensive Smells

While the majority of the family are various shades of brown, others show bright warning coloration of oranges, reds, and blacks. All species have fully developed wings as adults,

⤳ *In the tropical savanna of the* campo cerrado *region of Brazil* Machtima crucigera *inserts its rostrum into a vine stem in order to feed from the sap.*

⊙ Not all members of the family Coreidae are leaf-footed, as is evident in this individual of Leptocelis centralis, sitting on a heliconia flower in rain forest in Peru.

⊙ A male Laminiceps species leaf-footed bug sits on a leaf in rain forest in Argentina. It is one of the many species in which the hind femora are enlarged and bear a number of sharp spines.

and they all have the ability to produce unpleasant smells from glands in the thorax. The smells, together with the ability of some species to squirt unpleasant liquid from their rear ends, gives them some defense against their enemies. The whole family are plant feeders, and as a result some are pests.

The name "leaf-footed bug" relates to the structure of the hind tibiae. The alternative name of squash bug relates to one family member in North America being an important pest that feeds on and damages squashes, cucumbers, melons, gourds, pumpkins, and other members of the cucumber family. The culprit, *Anasa tristis,* was given the name of squash bug, and the name was then used to describe many other similar-looking bugs living in North America. From there the name has spread to other parts of the English-speaking world.

The Australian name of tip-wilter bug arose because many Coreidae damage the young, growing tips of the plants on which they feed. Nowadays scientists tend to use the name leaf-footed bug. Even that name, however, covers only a proportion of the family, since in some species part of the tarsus of the leg is expanded instead of the tibia. Those species are referred to as flag-footed bugs. Using the proper family name for any group is therefore better than trying to use common names, since they can be very confusing.

Friend or Foe

Apart from the squash bug, there are many other problem species in the family. *Amblypelta* species, for example, feed from the fruits of a number of important tropical trees, including cocoa. Controlling these pests has traditionally involved the use of insecticides, but a new idea is being tried out. The weaver ant, *Oecophylla smaragdina,* is a ferocious predator of *Amblypelta.* Placing colonies of the ants on test

The "Sultan" Bug

The mating behavior of the winter cherry bug, *Acanthocoris sordidus* from Japan, is quite unusual, since the males keep what in human terms would be described as a harem. The male winter cherry bug looks for a group of females gathered on their food plant. He then sets up a small territory around them, defending it from other males, just like an eastern potentate of old with his harem. Other males will attempt to take over the territory, which will result in the territory owner charging at them. Normally, even if the intruder is bigger, he will retreat from the onslaught of the territory-owning male. The situation remains the same as long as there are reasonably good supplies of food plants and females. However, when there is a shortage, things can change. The intruders will fight back; and if they are bigger, their chances of taking over the resident male's territory increase.

As far as both males and females are concerned, the less crowded the food plant is the better: Overcrowding means that the nymphs feed less well, and they finally molt into small adults. Small males are not as good at defending territories as larger ones.

trees has shown them to be effective in controlling the bugs.

In the New World various *Leptoglossus* species leaf-footed bugs are a problem. In North America, for example, the culprit is *L. occidentalis.* The bug feeds on the developing seeds of various conifers and, as a result, causes a reduction in the amount of seeds produced in commercial conifer seed nurseries. Unfortunately the bug seems to have made its way into Europe: In 1999 it was discovered on pines at a number of sites in northern Italy.

The peach palm or pupunha, *Bactris gasipaes,* has been grown in South America since long before the time when Europeans arrived there. When fully grown, it becomes multistemmed, and the hearts of those stems that do not fruit are an excellent food source for humans. More important, however, are the fruits, which can be cooked and eaten or can yield flour and oil. The palm is now grown over much of South and Central America as an important crop, although it does not occur in the wild. As is often the case when humans increase the numbers of a plant by growing it for food, the numbers of animals that feed on it also increase. One such animal is a leaf-footed bug, *Leptoglossus lonchoides.* It feeds on the developing peach palm fruits, damaging them to such an extent that they fall off, reducing the crop as a whole. The bug is now considered a serious pest.

On the other side of the coin are some leaf-footed bugs that are making a positive contribution by helping get rid of pests. Since the bugs are sap feeders, they are, of course, helping control plants

⊕ *Nymphs of the leaf-footed bug* Spartocera fusca *sit on a leaf in rain forest in Mexico. Their warning coloration indicates that they produce unpleasant secretions to ward off predators.*

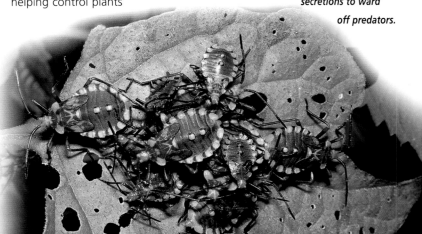

that are pests. *Mozena obtusa* feeds on the flower and leaf buds of honey mesquite, *Prosopis glandulosa*—a native of the desert Southwest of North America. The damage caused by the bug reduces the numbers of seeds produced and helps keep the tree in check naturally. The tree has been introduced into both South Africa and Australia, where, without any natural controls, it is spreading rapidly. Studies are being carried out to see if *Mozena obtusa* can be safely introduced into those countries to help control the mesquite.

In the wetlands of Florida another problem exists: The Australian paperbark tree, *Melaleuca quinquenervia*, is spreading uncontrollably. In Australia the tree is kept under control naturally by the tip-wilter bug, *Pomponatius typicus*. The

bugs feed on the young shoots of the tree, causing them to wilt and die so that the tree does not grow very quickly. When scientists are sure that it will not cause any problems in the state, the bug will probably be introduced into Florida with the aim of bringing the paperbark tree under control.

The Golden Egg Bug

The golden egg bug, *Phyllomorpha laciniata*, is found around the Mediterranean region, where it lives on *Paronychia* species plants. The plant has whorls of tiny green leaves between which are coils of silvery, paperlike bracts that themselves resemble leaves. The bug is rather unusual for several reasons. It is one of the smallest of the leaf-footed bugs and in fact looks more like a lace bug. It has no extensions of the hind tibiae, so it is not strictly leaf-footed, and it is an almost perfect mimic of the plant on which it lives.

Piggybacking Eggs

Females of the species are perhaps unique among the Coreidae in that they lay their eggs on the backs of other male and female bugs of their own species. Provided there are other males and females around, egg-laying females will lay eggs on them—otherwise they will lay them on the *Paronychia* food plant. More eggs are laid on the backs of males than on females, although it has been found that this has no effect on the survival rate of the eggs. Both males and females were found to lose quite a few of the eggs that they carry. The reason for more eggs being laid on males may be that if the male accepts the eggs, the female will allow him to mate with her.

Why do the females lay their eggs on the backs of other bugs? The answer relates to the fact that few of the eggs laid on the food plant survive to hatching, since most of them are either carried off as food by ants or fall victim to small parasitic wasps, which lay their own eggs inside them. Clearly, the egg-carrying bugs are successful in keeping the ants and the wasps away from the precious eggs.

⊙ *Nymph and adult members of the family Alydidae are often good ant mimics. The ant-mimicking nymph of* Mirperus jaculus *is on* Lantana camara *fruits in Kenya.*

Broad-Headed Bugs

The small family of broad-headed bugs (Alydidae) contains about 250 species worldwide and 29 in North America. They are similar in appearance to the Coreidae, but the main difference is the size of the head in relation to the width of the thorax. The broad-headed bug's head is always more than half the width of the rear edge of the pronotum, while in the leaf-footed bugs the head is always less than half the width of the pronotum, with just a few exceptions. Another feature that distinguishes them is the appearance of the fourth antennal segment. In broad-headed bugs it is slightly curved and longer than the third segment, while in leaf-footed bugs it is straight and shorter than the third segment. Broad-headed bugs are generally longer and slimmer, and leaf-footed bugs are usually shorter and broader—but there are exceptions.

Mimicry of other insects is common in the family. Adult *Alydus calcaratus* and *A. eurinus*, both from North America, mimic spider-hunting wasps in appearance and to a certain extent in behavior. They run around on the ground in a fussy sort of way, just like one of the wasps as it searches for a spider. The nymphs of the bugs, on the other hand, are perfect mimics of black ants, especially in the early instars. That type of mimicry is also found in the nymphs and even in the adults of many other species. Both adults and nymphs will, however, release unpleasant-smelling chemicals if their mimicry fails and they are attacked by a predator.

The family as a whole mainly feeds on seeds, especially on grasses or members of the pea and bean families. *Alydus calcaratus* is particularly fond of gorse seeds. Being seed and grass feeders means that at least some broad-headed bugs inevitably feed on the cultivated species on which humans rely. One of the worst culprits is the paddy bug, *Leptocorisa oratorius*, from Asia. All stages of the bug can damage the developing grains of rice and can reduce the crop yield by as much as 5 percent. It is therefore a great concern in countries where there is a shortage of food.

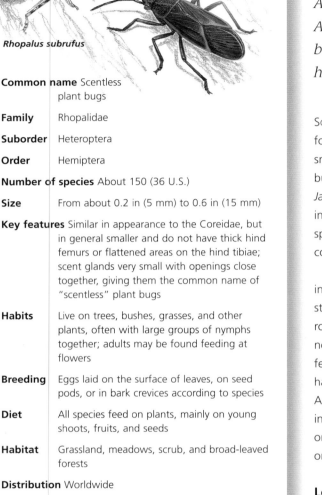

Eastern box elder bug
(*Boisea trivittata*)

Rhopalus subrufus

Common name Scentless plant bugs

Family Rhopalidae

Suborder Heteroptera

Order Hemiptera

Number of species About 150 (36 U.S.)

Size From about 0.2 in (5 mm) to 0.6 in (15 mm)

Key features Similar in appearance to the Coreidae, but in general smaller and do not have thick hind femurs or flattened areas on the hind tibiae; scent glands very small with openings close together, giving them the common name of "scentless" plant bugs

Habits Live on trees, bushes, grasses, and other plants, often with large groups of nymphs together; adults may be found feeding at flowers

Breeding Eggs laid on the surface of leaves, on seed pods, or in bark crevices according to species

Diet All species feed on plants, mainly on young shoots, fruits, and seeds

Habitat Grassland, meadows, scrub, and broad-leaved forests

Distribution Worldwide

⤒ *The eastern box elder bug,* Boisea trivittata, *is found on box elder trees in the United States. The eastward spread of the bug is attributed to the planting of box elder trees in parks and gardens. Length 0.5–0.6 inches (13–16 mm).* Rhopalus subrufus *is a scentless plant bug from Europe. Length 0.3–0.4 inches (8–10 mm).*

Scentless Plant Bugs

Rhopalidae

Although a fairly inconspicuous family, one North American member of the Rhopalidae—the box elder bug—has developed a habit of overwintering in houses, making a nuisance of itself in the process.

SCENTLESS PLANT BUGS LOOK very similar to leaf-footed bugs, although they are usually a bit smaller. In North America typical scentless plant bugs are the box elder bugs (see box) and the *Jadera* species—tropical bugs that have spread into Florida and Texas. In Europe typical-looking species are the *Rhopalus* species and the pretty coastal sand dune dweller, *Corizus hyoscyami.*

Jadera haematoloma is a common species in Florida. Unfortunately, when squashed, it can stain clothes, especially those of children as they roll around on the lawn. The bugs do not normally live on grass but may travel there to feed on the seeds of ornamental plants that have fallen onto lawns. In South and Central America *Jadera* nymphs often gather together in large groups. They are warningly colored (red or orange) and appear from a distance as a red or orange splash on a leaf or on tree bark.

Long and Thin

Less obviously members of the Rhopalidae are the long, thin *Chorosoma* and *Myrmus* species. They were originally thought to be from Europe and Asia, but *Chorosoma* bugs have turned up in Idaho, Oregon, and Nevada. *Chorosoma* species could almost be confused with walkingsticks, but they do not have their long thorax.

Myrmus species are smaller in size and not found in North America. *Myrmus miriformis* occurs in the British Isles. It lives in grassland, where it feeds mainly on unripe seeds. Males exist in two color forms—brown or green—with brown being commoner. They are normally partially winged but occasionally may be fully winged. The green females are fully winged.

⊙ *A group of warningly colored* Jadera obscura *nymphs on a palm leaf in the gloomy rain forest understory in Costa Rica.*

Box Elder Bugs

Box elder bugs are members of the Rhopalidae that come from North America. Their name derives from the fact that the main tree on which they feed is the box elder, or ash-leafed maple, *Acer negundo*. There are two different species of box elder bug, *Boisea trivittata* and *B. rubrolineata*, both originally from the West. *Boisea trivittata* has spread to the East in recent years, so that the two species are now given separate common names. *Boisea trivittata*, the commoner species, is called the eastern box elder bug, and *B. rubrolineata* is the western box elder bug. Part of the reason for the spread of the eastern bug is the planting of decorative forms of the tree in parks and gardens. In the wild the host tree is normally found along the sides of streams in broad-leaved forests.

Box elder bugs have also been recorded as feeding on other maples as well as cultivated fruit trees such as plum, cherry, and apple, and grapevines, where some damage to the fruit can occur. In exceptional cases the bug can reach very large numbers, with the result that there can be a considerable loss of leaves from the trees on which they are feeding.

During the fall large numbers of adult and nymphal box elder bugs congregate on their host trees before making their way to overwintering sites in suitable cracks and crevices. Unfortunately, such sites abound in human homes, and the bugs head for a nearby house—often in such large numbers that they become a nuisance. Indoors they may easily be squashed, producing a red stain.

⊝ *A group of adults of the eastern box elder bug,* **Boisea trivittata,** *on clematis flowers in Utah. Nymphs are found on various host trees, where they feed on sap.*

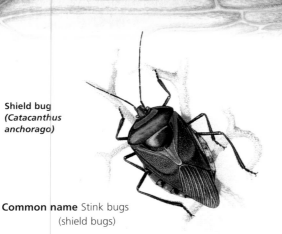

Shield bug
(*Catacanthus
anchorago*)

Common name Stink bugs
(shield bugs)

Family   Pentatomidae

Suborder Heteroptera

Order   Hemiptera

Number of species About 5,000 (222 U.S.)

Size   From about 0.2 in (4 mm) to 1 in (2.5 cm)

Key features Broad-bodied, often oval-shaped bugs,
nearly as wide as they are long; often rather
flattened on top; scutellum is usually
triangular, extending over as much as half the
abdomen but not overlapping the
membranous area of the forewings by much;
front of the pronotum may have blunt or
pointed projections on either side of the
head; stink glands present

Habits   Most often found on the plants on which
they feed; predaceous species found on any
suitable vegetation in search of prey

Breeding In a number of species the females care for
their eggs and young; in many species males
stridulate to attract females

Diet   Many are sap feeders; others feed on insects,
especially soft-bodied ones such as larvae

Habitat Meadows, grassland, forests, sand dunes,
seashore, marshes, and deserts

Distribution Worldwide, but tropical zones are especially
rich in species

⬆ *The bright colors of the shield bug* Catacanthus
anchorago *from Asia give a clear indication to would-be
predators that the bug contains foul-tasting defensive
chemicals and gives off equally unpleasant smells. Length
about 0.5 inches (13 mm).*

Stink Bugs   Pentatomidae

*With such a large family, it is difficult to travel
far in virtually any habitat without coming
across a member of the Pentatomidae. The
brightly colored species are easy to pick out,
but many are well camouflaged and are
not at all easy to discern against their
natural background.*

WHATEVER THEIR COLOR, stink bugs are fairly easy
to recognize. Their proportions are such that,
on average, they are about twice as long as
they are broad, and looked at from the side
they are usually rather flat on top. Members of
related families tend to have a more rounded
top to the abdomen. As their alternative
common name of shield bugs indicates, the
scutellum is quite large, normally reaching to at
least halfway down the abdomen.

Giant shield bugs are very similar, except
that their head is small in relation to the rest of
the body, while the head of stink bugs is a
perfect match for the size of their body. It is not
uncommon for the sides of the front part of the
pronotum to be extended outward in various
ways. Those of the North American spined
soldier bugs (*Podisus* species) and the European
two-spined stink bug, *Picromerus bidens*, for
example, form sharp points.

Adult shield bugs are always winged, but
members of the genus *Lojus*, from Central and
South America, are rather unusual. They have a
pair of forewings, but the membranous hind
wings are absent, and therefore these bugs are
unable to fly.

Why "Stink Bugs"?

The reason for the name stink bug is that the
insects produce unpleasant smells to ward off
their enemies. The smelly chemicals come from
glands in the thorax of adult stink bugs and
the abdomen of the nymphs. The chemicals
also make the bugs taste unpleasant, so that

⬆ *Feeding on sap
running through the
stem of a plant in the
Peruvian rain forest is an
adult* Peromatus *species
stink bug. Members of
the Pentatomidae tend to
have flatter backs than
other related families.*

➡ *A pair of stink bugs,*
Edessa rufomarginata,
*mating as they sit on a
leaf in the rain forest of
Peru. Tail-to-tail mating is
normal, and the female
is the larger of the
two bugs.*

would-be predators avoid them once they have learned how disgusting they are. The unpleasant fluids are released through openings on the underside of the body, and the bugs may lift their abdomen up in the air to expose their underside when releasing them. The smell they produce can be very noticeable. The European green shield bug, *Palomena prasina*, for example, can be very common in gardens and often gets caught up in lawn mowers. The strong smell produced as a result can pervade the area for several feet around.

Adults of the stink bug *Cosmopepla bimaculata* have been examined in detail to find out more about how the bug emits its unpleasant fluids. It appears that the bugs have the ability to produce the fluid from the left or right glands, or both at the same time. They can also control how much fluid is produced, What is more, if it is not used, they can withdraw it back into the gland from which it was produced, avoiding any waste. The fluid is obviously very effective in deterring potential predators. Under experimental conditions a variety of different bird species, as well as anole lizards, rejected the bugs when they were offered them.

Like the caterpillars of many species of Lepidoptera, stink bugs have been found to obtain the defensive chemicals from the plants on which they feed. The North American harlequin bug, *Murgantia histrionica*, feeds on a range of plants from the cabbage family and is a pest of cultivated varieties. Although eaten by humans, cabbages tend to have a very strong smell, especially when they are going bad. That is because the plants contain substances called mustard oils, which deter some creatures from eating them. The harlequin bug is able to concentrate the mustard oils so that in its body they are 20 to 30 times as strong as they are in the plant. When the harlequin bugs were presented to several different species of birds, they were not prepared to eat them.

Helpful Bacteria

The majority of stink bugs feed on plant sap. In order for them to be able to make use of it, they enlist the help of special bacteria that live in small pockets in the side of the gut. The bacteria are absolutely essential, so female bugs smear their eggs with their own droppings, which contain the bacteria. When the young hatch out, they are able to take in the bacteria provided by their mother.

Members of the subfamily Amyoteinae take small animal prey, especially caterpillars or other slow-moving insects of a suitable size, and occasionally suck sap if they are hungry. Feeding mainly on animals means that they do not need bacteria to assist them. Predatory stink bugs appear to be very tolerant of some of the chemicals found in their prey: They are often found feeding on ladybugs or moth larvae, which contain substances that make insectivorous birds and mammals ill.

Timid Hunters

Sap feeders tend to have a narrow rostrum, but in the predatory species it is somewhat thicker. The latter are rather timid in their approach to prey. They wander around, reaching forward with their sensitive antennae for anything suitable. On contacting the prey, they gently push their stylets into it. If it reacts too violently, they pull them out and back off rapidly. However, if the prey is not too aggressive, the stylets spread out inside the prey's body so that it is unable to pull itself off. As the bug injects digestive juices, the prey becomes immobile, and it is then usually sucked dry.

Some species of predatory stink bug are quite important in helping control pests—for

⊛ *Some stink bugs are predaceous, but they tend to feed on soft-bodied prey.* Oplomus dichrous *from Mexico digs its proboscis into an unfortunate moth caterpillar.*

Plataspid Stink Bugs

The mainly tropical African and Asian family Plataspidae, related to the Pentatomidae, has no accepted common name. By virtue of the fact that they look very much like beetles, they could perhaps be called "beetle bugs," although that could be confusing. The reason for their beetlelike appearance is that they are flattened on the underside. Also, the scutellum is very large and curves over the abdomen, covering it completely. The easiest way to tell them apart is to look for the line down the center of the back, which separates the two wing cases in beetles. Since the scutellum is a single structure, the line is not present in plataspid stink bugs.

These bugs may be brightly colored and are often very shiny, as if they had been polished. Some species form groups of adults and nymphs, with the adults warningly colored while the nymphs are camouflaged. In some species the males have a pair of "horns" sticking out of the front of the head between the eyes; horns are not found in the females. All species are plant feeders, and one or two may reach pest proportions on certain pulse crops.

One species has been noted as having an interesting relationship with ants. *Caternaultiella rugosa*, from Cameroon in West Africa, lives in groups at the base of a particular species of tree. The ants build shelters—called pavilions—over the bugs and their eggs to hide the eggs from the attentions of female parasitic wasps. The pavilions are not always big enough, meaning that some bugs are left outside. The egg masses and the nymphs inside the pavilions are then deserted by the females and left in the care of the ants. Outside the pavilions, however, the female bugs continue to look after any eggs that were left out and the first instar nymphs. What is more, adults and final instar nymphs form protective groups around the first instar nymphs.

Left: Plataspid stink bugs resemble beetles, as seen in Ceratocoris cephalicus from Uganda. The male has long "horns."
Inset: Adults and nymphs are easy to distinguish in these Libyaspis coccinelloides plataspid stink bugs from Madagascar. The adults are striped and warningly colored, while the nymphs are camouflaged.

example, the eyed stink bug, *Perillus bioculatus*, which is widespread throughout North America. It is a major predator of larvae of the Colorado potato beetle, *Leptinotarsa decemlineata*. As a result of its success in controlling that pest, it has been introduced into Europe to see if it can carry out the same level of control there.

While the eyed stink bug is warningly colored, there are other useful North American predatory stink bugs that use camouflage. The *Brochymena* species live on trees, including those in orchards, where they feed on caterpillars and other soft-bodied insects. Their coloration is almost a perfect match for the bark of the trees on which they live.

Although the eyed stink bug should be encouraged, there are a number of stink bugs that are undesirable, since they feed on and

⊙ *Giant stink bug nymphs are often an unusual shape. This is a group of Lyramorpha species nymphs from Australia, their bright-red color indicating that they are probably distasteful.*

⊙ *Oncomeris flavicornis from the dense tropical rain forests of New Guinea is one of the largest species of tessaratomids. It is a powerful flier and emits a loud buzz.*

Giant Shield Bugs

The small family Tessaratomidae, with around 260 species, comes mainly from Southeast Asia and Australasia. A few species are known to live in the tropics of the New World. They are large insects, with adults of some species reaching 1.5 inches (4 cm) in length. They are similar in appearance to stink bugs, but they differ from them in the relationship between the size of the head and that of the body. In stink bugs the head looks the right size for the body, while in giant shield bugs the head looks too small for such a large body.

Another feature of the giant shield bugs is their nymphs, which can assume quite bizarre shapes when compared with the normally rather rounded stink bug nymphs. Those of the giant shield bugs may be rectangular, triangular, or even kite shaped and may have very pretty colors and markings.

One species in Australia is gaining notoriety. The bronze orange bug, *Musgraveia sulciventris*, has become something of a pest on citrus trees. (Its common name is derived from a combination of its main color—bronze—and its habitat—orange trees.) Both adults and nymphs feed from the young shoots of the citrus trees and can cause considerable damage in commercial orchards. The species has another unpleasant habit: If disturbed, it squirts out a foul-smelling brown liquid that can burn the skin and cause extreme discomfort if it gets into the eyes of predators or humans.

Burrower Bugs

The burrower bugs in the family Cydnidae are sometimes included with the stink bugs of the family Pentatomidae. However, they are perhaps best considered as a family in their own right, if only because of the unusual lifestyle of most species. They may grow up to 0.6 inches (15 mm) in length but are usually less than 0.4 inches (10 mm). They have the typical broad body of a stink bug or shield bug, but the most obvious features that distinguish them from related families are the heavily spined legs that they use for burrowing. They sometimes burrow as deep as 3 feet (9 m) in order for the females to lay their eggs in the soil. Nymphs of all but a few species then feed from plant roots.

A slightly less typical burrower bug, but one that is most likely to be seen, is *Sehirus* species. The reason it is not so typical is that the nymphs feed above the ground. *Sehirus bicolor* from Europe uses mainly the white deadnettle, *Lamium album*, as its food plant. The female still digs into the ground to form a chamber in which to lay her eggs, but the nymphs climb up onto the deadnettle to feed after hatching. *Sehirus cinctus* from North America feeds on *Stachys palustris*, but the female of the species has an extra trick up her sleeve. Like *S. bicolor*, she lays her eggs in the soil. But when the nymphs hatch, she carries seeds down from the plant for them to feed on. Only after they have molted into the second instar do they then emerge from the soil and climb onto the plant to feed.

The female of the Asian burrower bug, *Parastrachia japonensis*, goes even further. From the tree on which she lives she "picks" a fruit on the end of her rostrum. She then climbs down to the ground, digs a nest chamber, and lays her eggs. When the nymphs hatch, they feed from the fruit that she has so carefully provided for them. She eventually leads her second instar nymphs onto the leaf litter above the nest chamber, where they continue to feed on fruits that have fallen from the host tree.

One European burrower bug exhibits a kind of parental care that is very rare among bugs as a whole. Females of *Brachypelta aterrima* produce special secretions from the end of the gut, a sort of "baby food" on which the first instar nymphs feed. At the same time, the nymphs take in special bacteria that will help them digest their food throughout the rest of their life.

damage human crops. The harlequin cabbage bug or calico bug, *Murgantia histrionica*—another North American species—is a good example. It feeds on all sorts of plants of the cabbage family, leaving pale marks on the leaves and making the crop unsellable. The green vegetable bug, *Nezara viridula*, is even more of a problem: It is very common in the warmer parts of the world and attacks many crops, including tomatoes and various pulses.

Courtship Concerts

Some stink bugs stridulate, producing "songs" to attract members of the opposite sex. The songs are produced by scraping a row of pegs on the femur of the hind leg against a ridged area beneath the abdomen. Stridulation in a European species, the woundwort stink bug, *Eysarcoris fabricii*, can sometimes bring the sexes together in their hundreds. Humans are unable to hear the songs made by the bugs, but with the use of electronic equipment they can be picked up and recorded.

The green vegetable bug, *Nezara viridula,* demonstrates a complex use of song. A pheromone produced by the male is responsible for the initial gathering of the bugs. Once gathered together, the "singing" can commence. Scientists have found that the female bugs have three distinct songs, while the males can produce seven, although three of them are very similar. Rival males duet with each other, while males and females also sing to one another. Once a suitable pair get together, courtship begins. Courtship itself can

⤺ *In England a male pied shield bug, Sehirus bicolor (left)—a burrower bug—head-butts the underside of a female in an attempt to make her accept him as a mate.*

⤒ *A group of woundwort stink bugs, Eysarcoris fabricii, in England. They have been brought together by the stridulation of the males, and the group includes both single bugs and mating pairs.*

be quite complicated and may involve various actions. Males, for example, may tap or stroke the females with their antennae, and the females may respond by jerking their body up and down. Mating finally takes place with the sexes joined tail to tail and facing in opposite directions. In general, females are bigger than males, and it is not unusual to see a mating male being dragged unceremoniously backward as the female continues with her daily routine.

Pheromones are also used by many other species of stink bug to attract members of the opposite sex, an example being the males of *Thyanta pallidovirens*. Researchers have discovered, however, that this does not always result in a totally happy outcome—not only does the pheromone attract female bugs, but it also attracts female sphecid (solitary) wasps. The *Astata occidentalis* wasp provisions her nest with the stink bug for her larvae to feed on. It is likely that the female stink bug, attracted by the male's scent, will find that he has been taken by the time she arrives.

The Egg Burster

Stink bug eggs are normally laid in small groups and are often found stuck to the underside of a leaf. They are usually pale at first; but as the nymph develops inside, they darken. Once they are fully developed, the first instar nymphs use an "egg burster" to escape from the shell. The egg burster is a "t"-shaped tooth situated on the head. The first instar nymphs often stay together for a while before wandering off to feed. In certain tropical stink bugs the newly hatched nymphs cluster around the empty eggshells. In that state they resemble a hairy, stinging caterpillar. Another advantage is that, if molested by a predator, their combined chemical defenses are roughly equivalent to those of an adult bug.

⊛ *Newly hatched nymphs of a* **Peromatus** *species stink bug sit around the empty eggshells from which they have recently emerged. In this pose they are thought to resemble a stinging caterpillar and are therefore unlikely to be molested by predators, especially birds.*

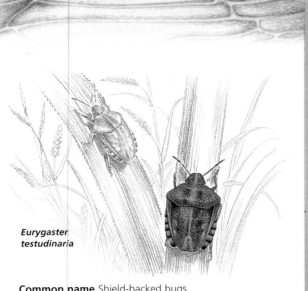

Eurygaster
testudinaria

Common name Shield-backed bugs

Family Scutelleridae

Suborder Heteroptera

Order Hemiptera

Number of species About 400 (34 U.S.)

Size From about 0.3 in (9 mm) to 0.8 in (20 mm) or more

Key features Broad-bodied, often oval-shaped bugs nearly as wide as they are long; similar shape as stink bugs, but usually not as flat on top; scutellum is large, covering most of the membranous area of the forewings; look very similar to beetles; colors range from browns and greens to bright metallic hues

Habits Usually found sitting and feeding from their host plants

Breeding Maternal care occurs in the family; eggs laid on food plants

Diet All species suck sap from their host plants; a number are crop pests

Habitat Meadows, grassland, forests, sand dunes, seashore, marshes, and deserts

Distribution Worldwide, but more common in tropical zones

⊕ **Eurygaster testudinaria** *is found in Europe and Asia. It prefers damp situations, such as marshy areas with tall vegetation, where it feeds on sedges and rushes. Length 0.3–0.4 inches (9–11 mm).*

Shield-Backed Bugs

Scutelleridae

With their rather rounded backs and shiny, metallic appearance some shield-backed bugs might be mistaken for beetles. However, the presence of a rostrum rather than biting jaws immediately characterizes them as bugs.

THE MOST OBVIOUS FEATURE that separates the Scutelleridae from the closely related stink bugs (Pentatomidae) and shield bugs (Acanthosomatidae) is the size of the scutellum—the hard plate covering the thorax. In shield-backed bugs the structure extends so far back from the rear edge of the pronotum that it covers most, if not all, of the wings. The scutellum is most developed in bugs such as *Eurygaster alternatus* from North America and the very similar European tortoise bug, *E. maura*. Rather than the usual triangular shape, the scutellum in these two species has parallel sides and a rounded end. It reaches to the end of the abdomen and almost completely covers the wings. However, some Pentatomidae also have a scutellum that extends back to the end of the abdomen—for example, the minstrel

⊕ *A group of nymphs of the Australian harlequin bug,* Tectocoris diophthalmus, *from different instars. The pale individuals have just molted their old cuticles.*

⊕ *Eurygaster maura, the European tortoise bug, feeds on a wide range of plants. In continental Europe it can be a pest on various cereal crops.*

bug, *Graphosoma italicum*, from Europe. Close examination reveals that, unlike in the shield-backed bugs, in stink bugs the scutellum either does not have parallel sides, or (if it does) there are hooks on the pronotum beside the eyes.

Crop Pests

Members of this mainly tropical family are all plant feeders, and they are perhaps best known for the fact that some of them are pests of cultivated crops. In Europe and Asia, for example, the sunn pest, *Eurygaster integriceps*, causes serious damage to cereal crops. A great deal of research is being carried out to try to control its numbers.

Some shield-backed bugs are very colorful. The *Tectocoris* species harlequin bugs from Australia are a good example, with bright reds, oranges, and metallic blues. However, they can cause damage to cotton crops in that country.

Pachycoris kluggi from South America has been found to exhibit parental care. Females have been observed to protect both their eggs and nymphs from the attentions of other insects, especially parasitic wasps.

⤵ *A female parent bug, Elasmucha grisea (Acanthosomatidae), guards a pile of her newly hatched nymphs on the leaf of a birch tree in England.*

Shield Bugs

Shield bugs in the family Acanthosomatidae are closely related to the shield-backed bugs and sometimes included with them in the stink bug family Pentatomidae. In some reference books the family is called the Acanthosomidae. They can be distinguished from the other families by the fact that there are only two segments to the tarsus of each leg rather than three. All members of the family are sap feeders, living mainly on shrubs and trees.

Perhaps the most interesting members of the family are the *Elasmucha* species from North America, Europe, and Asia in which the females care for their eggs and larvae. The parent bug, *Elasmucha grisea,* a European species that lives on birch trees, has been widely studied. As its common name indicates, the females are excellent mothers. They lay their batches of 30 to 40 eggs so that most of them are covered by their own body. During the 20 or so days that it takes for the eggs to hatch, the females take tiny meals by probing the cells of the leaf on which the eggs have been laid. At first they are keeping off tiny parasitic wasps, which attempt to lay their eggs inside the bug eggs. Once the eggs hatch, the females guard the young from other predatory insects and even birds, raising their wings and producing a rather unpleasant smell when danger threatens. They herd their young around the twig on which they live, moving to a new feeding area once the old one has run out of food. The females stay with their young until they become adult.

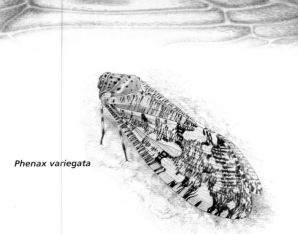

Phenax variegata

Common name Lanternflies
(fulgorid bugs, fulgorid
planthoppers)

Family Fulgoridae

Suborder Auchenorrhyncha

Order Hemiptera

Number of species About 700 (at least 1 U.S.)

Size From about 0.4 in (10 mm) to 4 in (10 cm)

Key features Both fore- and hind wings covered in a
complicated network of veins and cross-veins;
many (especially tropical) species have strange
growths from the front of the head,
sometimes knobbed or spiny; color may be
plain browns or greens, or sometimes very
colorful

Habits Like most plant feeders, they sit motionless
on their host plant to escape detection by
predators

Breeding Some species produce sounds during
courtship; females of some species lay eggs
into the ground

Diet Sap from their host plant species

Habitat Mainly forests

Distribution Usually found in the tropics; a few species in
temperate zones

⊕ *The lanternfly* Phenax variegata *from South America
roosts on lichen-covered bark, which it resembles. It often
has long filaments of wax protruding from the end of the
abdomen. Length up to 1 inch (2.5 cm).*

Lanternflies

Fulgoridae

*The strange growths protruding from the front of the
head of many lanternflies and the amazing colors and
patterns on their wings make them some of the most
interesting looking of insects.*

ALTHOUGH SOME LANTERNFLIES ARE bizarre looking,
some are just plain brown in color, and many
do not have the outlandish head extensions of
some members of the family. Even some that
do have them are not brightly colored. The
head extensions are very variable—the peanut
pod-shaped structure on the head of the
peanut-head bug, *Fulgora laternaria* from the
American tropics, is perhaps the strangest of all.
Other shapes include sawlike structures or
curved extensions with bobbles on the end.

Whatever their shape, the reason for their
presence is puzzling. The most likely
explanation is that they are to deter intelligent
predators, such as birds, which might otherwise
consider the bugs to be a tasty meal. It is also
possible that a bird may be fooled into
believing that the head extension is
the bug's tail. The bird

⊙ *This* **Cathedra serrata**
*lanternfly from Brazil has
just been disturbed by
the photographer and
has flicked open its
wings in a startle display.
To a small-brained
predator it now looks
like the face of a much
larger creature, which the
predator should
avoid.*

will attack the rounded end of the wings instead, which are rather more head-shaped. The bird then simply gets a beak full of bits of wing, while the lanternfly uses what is left of its wings to fly off and make good its escape. It is equally possible that the overall shape of the "long-nosed" lanternflies is a good enough

disguise in itself and that the birds do not recognize them as insects at all.

Not only do lanternflies have strange head projections, but they also often have beautifully marked and colored wings, sometimes with large eyespots on them. Unfortunately, their beauty is resulting in a new trend that may

Ⓓ *A* Pyrops *species lanternfly adult sits on a tree in rain forest in Sumatra. The function of the long snout, with its bright-yellow knob, is not known.*

Flatid Planthoppers

Planthoppers in the family Flatidae are close relations of the lanternflies and, like them, are found mainly in the tropics and subtropics. More than 1,000 species have been described. They feed on the sap of a wide variety of plants. When at rest, they sit with their blunt-ended forewings held side by side almost vertically above the body. They vary in size from small species measuring just 0.16 inches (4 mm) long to large tropical species up to 1.3 inches (3.2 cm) in length.

The few species found in the warm, temperate areas of the world tend to be green or brown, but many tropical species are brightly colored. Both adults and nymphs can be found feeding together in large groups. The nymphs are quite striking because they have long strands of white wax protruding from their bodies. The wax, produced from the body surface, is unpleasant to taste and helps keep away predators. Rather unexpectedly, however, in Madagascar some of the forest geckos that feed on insects have been seen stimulating flatid bugs to produce honeydew, which they then drink.

There are 33 species in North America, and four in southern Europe. One species, *Metcalfa pruinosa*, is causing something of a problem in southern Europe. It was accidentally introduced from North America into Italy in 1979 and had spread into France by 1986. It feeds on over 100 different plant species, including a wide variety of ornamental trees and shrubs. It also feeds on fruit trees, where it can cause considerable damage as it feeds on the sap.

In its home range the species is perhaps less of a problem, since it has natural enemies to control it, but it can still be a pest in citrus orchards. In Europe its lack of natural enemies is causing the problem there.

Inset: Even when looking at them closely, the nymphs of the flatid planthopper Phromnia rosea, *a Madagascan species, do not look like insects at all. Instead, they resemble flowers with split and fraying petals.*
Far right: The adult group of Phromnia rosea *also looks remarkably like a cluster of flowers, pink ones in this instance.*

Delphacid Planthoppers

Although related to the lanternflies, the delphacid planthoppers in the family Delphacidae actually look more like leafhoppers of the family Cicadellidae. They are most easily distinguished from the leafhoppers, however, by the fact that they all have a jointed spur—like a spike—sticking out from the end of the tibia nearest the body. The family has around 1,700 species worldwide. They are mainly brown or green, which relates to the fact that most of them live on grasses and sedges.

As a result, there are a number of very important pest species that feed on cultivated grasses such as rice, corn, and sugarcane. The Asian brown planthopper, *Nilaparvarta lugens*, causes the disease "grass stunt" in rice across much of Asia and the Pacific rice-growing areas. Corn around the world is infected by a virus carried by the cornhopper, *Peregrinus maidis*, which also damages the seeds as it feeds. The Australian sugarcane hopper, *Perkinsiella saccharicida*, has now been spread around to most sugarcane-growing areas of the world. Unfortunately, it carries a very damaging virus known as Fiji disease. In some areas the pest is being successfully controlled by a predaceous plant bug, *Tytthus mundulus*.

eventually threaten some of the rarer species: Fixed specimens of lanternflies, displaying their beautiful markings, are now appearing for sale on the Internet in increasing numbers, presumably attracting customers who collect pinned butterflies and moths. Most are certainly collected in the wild, but what effect that will have on their future existence is uncertain.

Moth Targets

The lanternflies, as well as some bugs in the other planthopper families and occasionally cicadas, are the victims of one particular family of moths. Moths usually feed on nectar as adults and chew leaves as caterpillars. However, moths of the small family Epipyropidae, most of which come from the tropics of the Southern Hemisphere, have parasitic caterpillars whose main hosts are lanternflies. The moth caterpillars live on the outside of the bugs'

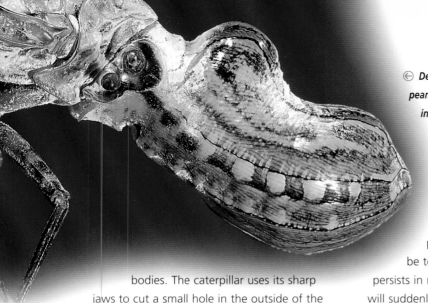

bodies. The caterpillar uses its sharp jaws to cut a small hole in the outside of the lanternfly and then feeds on the body fluids that ooze out. Sometimes the caterpillar has little or no effect on its host; but at other times the host may die once the caterpillar has finished feeding.

Peanut-Head Bug

Of all the unusual-looking fulgorids the peanut-head (or just peanut) bug, *Fulgora laternaria*, is one of the most bizarre. It gets its name from the unusual growth on the front of its head, which is shaped like a peanut pod. It was once believed that the "peanut" on the front of the head glowed in the dark, but that is now known to be untrue. The name "lanternfly" originated from this belief. The rest of the family also then became known as lanternflies. The bug is found throughout Central and South America, and is well-known by the local people, who call it the *machaca*. There is a popular belief that if a girl is stung by a machaca, then she must sleep with her partner within 24 hours; otherwise she is certain to die. Such beliefs cannot be based on fact, since peanut-head bugs do not sting.

The peanut-head bug is a big insect, around 3 inches (7.6 cm) long with a wing span of around 6 inches (15 cm). The bug sits along the trunk or branches of its host tree, feeding through its long rostrum, which measures between 0.6 and 0.8 inches (15 to 20 mm). It can therefore get through the bark to the living tissues beneath in order to feed. Sitting still in such a position and with its colors matching

those of the bark, it is very difficult for would-be predators to spot. With its long head projection the bug looks rather like a lizard—a fact that may also put off birds that would otherwise be tempted to attack it. If an attacker persists in molesting it, the peanut-head adult will suddenly fly off, at the same time releasing an unpleasant, skunklike smell. If that fails to deter the enemy, the bug then opens its wings, revealing two large eyespots. In the gloom of the forest it looks like the great big face of a much larger animal—enough to drive off all but the most persistent of attackers.

Other lanternfly species also have eyespots, but they are perhaps not quite so spectacular. The peanut-head bug has also been observed to have one further behavior that may help drive away its enemies: If disturbed, it will drum its head against the trunk of the tree on which it is sitting.

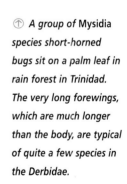

Short-Horned Bugs

The family of short-horned bugs—the Derbidae—is one of a number of families that at one time or another have been included in the lanternfly family, the Fulgoridae. Of the 800 or more described species the majority are from the tropics or subtropics, although 47 species are found in North America, one of which ranges as far north as Canada.

The head is small in relation to the body, the antennae are short and flattened, and the compound eyes can be quite large. Under the microscope a unique feature of the family can be seen: The segment forming the end of the rostrum is no longer than its width. In other families it is longer than it is wide. The delicate wings are highly patterned with veins, and the front pair varies from being transparent to highly colored. The wings of some species can be up to three times the length of the body. While in many species the wings are held together over the body, others sit with the wings held out to the side so that to some extent they resemble moths. Some species stridulate by rubbing together roughened areas of the wings, making sounds that can be heard by humans.

Living as many do in tropical forests and having such delicate wings, heavy rain can be a problem to them. The bugs have overcome the problem in a number of ways. The mothlike species, which are in most danger, sit beneath the large leaves of the plants on which they feed, often in large numbers. The leaves act as umbrellas and offer them some protection. Others sit at such an angle that the rain falls onto their head rather than onto their wings. Another group of short-horned bugs rolls their wings up into a tube and sits at an angle of 45 degrees to the leaf or stem on which they are perched, reducing the wing area that is exposed to the falling rain.

The adult bugs feed on a variety of plants, especially palms and grasses. Less is known about the nymphs of the family. They have been found living beneath the bark of trees and in rotten wood, where it is believed they feed on fungi. In *Cedusa inflata*, whose adults are common on palms in Florida and around the Caribbean, the nymphs were found in piles of organic debris on the ground beneath coconut palms. The nymphs were in the damper parts toward the center of the piles, usually close to the fungus mass, adding weight to the idea that the nymphs are mainly fungus feeders. In order to avoid wetting their delicate bodies, nymphs living in rotten wood line their tunnels with a wax that they produce themselves.

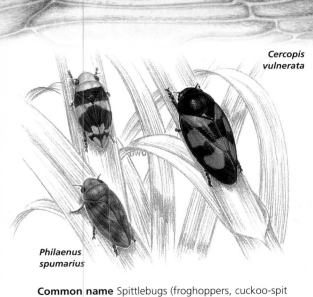

Cercopis vulnerata

Philaenus spumarius

Common name	Spittlebugs (froghoppers, cuckoo-spit insects)
Family	Cercopidae
Suborder	Auchenorrhyncha
Order	Hemiptera
Number of species	About 2,400 (54 U.S.)
Size	From about 0.12 in (3 mm) to 0.8 in (20 mm)
Key features	Rather squat body shaped like a miniature frog, with powerful hind legs for jumping long distances in relation to body size; either brownish or with bright warning colors; forewings leathery and colored; tibiae cylindrical (unlike the similar-looking leafhoppers, which have tibiae with an angular cross section); nymphs easily recognizable, living in a mass of froth
Habits	Normally found sitting on food plants; many adults not noticeable unless they jump
Breeding	Females lay eggs in crevices on or near food plants, or directly into soil; some produce protective secretion around eggs
Diet	Some adults feed from parts of plants growing above ground, as do many nymphs; others feed from plant roots
Habitat	Meadows, gardens, grassland, moors, forests, mountains, and deserts
Distribution	Worldwide, with many temperate species

⏶ *The meadow spittlebug,* Philaenus spumarius, *is found in North America and Europe. Shown above are two of the 11 color variations. Length about 0.2 inches (5–6 mm).* Cercopis vulnerata *is from Europe. Length 0.3–0.4 inches (9–11 mm).*

Spittlebugs

Cercopidae

The common name of spittlebug is given to the Cercopidae because of their ability to produce a frothy substance from their abdomen in which the nymphs hide. They are also very good at jumping, which gives them their alternative common name of froghopper.

AS WITH MOST OTHER insects, the ability of the spittlebugs to jump is because the hind legs are strongly developed. Adult spittlebugs are fully winged, with the forewings longer and tougher than the more delicate hind wings. The wings are held like a tent over the body when at rest. Many species have camouflage colors of subdued browns, grays, and greens, while others, especially tropical species, may have bright warning coloration.

One species, *Philaenus spumarius* (known as the meadow spittlebug in North America and the common froghopper in the British Isles), which is common both in North America and Europe, has 11 distinct color patterns. It seems that the bugs with darker patterns survive better in dirty, polluted environments, while the paler forms are common in the cleaner countryside.

Frothy Hideaway

Spittlebugs are often seen sitting side by side in pairs, which is the normal mating position for the family. Females lay their eggs in crevices on or near the food plants or, in the case of those whose nymphs live on roots, in the soil. *Philaenus spumarius* produces a white secretion around her eggs that then becomes hard and helps the eggs survive the winter. On hatching, the young nymphs make their way to the food plant and

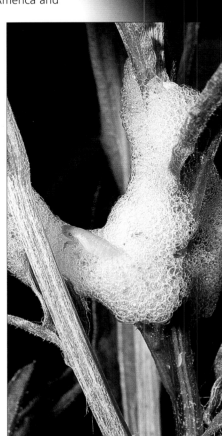

begin to feed. Those that live on stems sit with their head pointing downward as they feed. There is a good reason for that: The sap from the plant contains far more water than the bugs need for their own use, so it is passed out of the end of the abdomen. As it goes, it is mixed with a special secretion from glands in the abdomen. The mixture forms the froth in which the nymphs hide, and which is the "spit" or "spittle" that gives the insects their common name of spittlebug.

Even though they are protected by the soil, nymphs that feed from roots still produce a mass of spit. While nymphs of *P. spumarius* live alone in their spit, those of other species may feed close to one another and form a single, dripping mass of froth. Just before the fifth and final instar nymph is ready to molt its skin to become an adult, it produces an extralarge bubble of air, which blows the froth off its body. The action allows the newly emerged adult to harden its skin while exposed to the air—a necessity for most insects.

While the froth certainly hides the nymphs from view, it is not a perfect form of protection. Some birds discover that there is something tasty inside the spit and learn to pull out the nymphs. A number of hunting wasps use the nymphs as food for their own grubs. They dive into the froth, pull out the nymph, give themselves a quick clean to remove any spit that has stuck to them, and then fly back to their nest with their prize.

"Cuckoo Spit"

The origin of "cuckoo spit," the common name in the British Isles for the froth produced by spittlebug nymphs, actually has nothing to do with cuckoos spitting. It does, however, have something to do with cuckoos: The common cuckoo of Europe and Asia is a migratory bird that spends the cold winter months in Africa. It returns north to the British Isles in spring at roughly the same time as the first hatching of spittlebug nymphs takes place. In former times when people heard the first cuckoos calling in spring and saw the first of the spittlebug spit, they put the two together and decided that the cuckoos must have produced it.

Just visible among the mass of froth, or "cuckoo spit," is a green nymph of the meadow spittlebug, Philaenus spumarius.

Tibicen plebejus

Common name Cicadas

Family Cicadidae

Suborder Auchenorrhyncha

Order Hemiptera

Number of species About 1,500 (160 U.S.)

Size From about 0.4 in (10 mm) to 4 in (10 cm)

Key features Mainly large insects; both pairs of wings membranous and transparent, held over the body like a tent; males have sound-producing structures beneath the front end of the abdomen; body often green or brown and well camouflaged

Habits Most species live in trees or bushes from which males call to females; nymphs live beneath the ground and are not seen until they emerge to molt into adults; adults fly strongly

Breeding Male cicadas have a distinct "song" to attract females of their own species; females insert eggs into twigs

Diet Adults take sap from the trees on which they live; nymphs take sap from tree roots

Habitat Mainly forests and woodlands; also in deserts where suitable woody plants grow

Distribution Worldwide, but more common in tropical zones

⊕ *Cicadas are sometimes kept in Asia for their song, as they were in ancient Greece. They are common around the Mediterranean region, where they favor pine trees. Tibicen plebejus, a European species, is around 1.2–1.5 inches (3–3.7 cm) in length.*

Cicadas

Cicadidae

While the nights in the tropics are often filled with the sounds of crickets, katydids, and frogs calling, the daylight hours usually resound with the raucous calls of thousands of male cicadas.

THE CICADAS ARE PERHAPS the most instantly recognizable of bugs because of their usually large size and the noise made by the males. The short, triangular head bears a pair of large compound eyes that aid them in flight. Both males and females have hearing organs on the abdomen, while males have a pair of sound-producing organs on the underside of the base of the abdomen. The forewings are much longer than the hind wings and extend well beyond the end of the body. Both pairs of wings may be transparent; in some species the forewings may be strikingly marked and colored. The body is often green, brown, or cryptically marked, making them difficult to pick out against the leaves or bark on which they usually perch. The hind legs are not developed for jumping as in related families.

Digging Nymphs

Adults feed on the sap of their host plant, but there are a number of species that do not feed at all as adults. Cicada nymphs have the front legs modified for digging, since they live beneath the ground, where they feed from the roots of their host plant.

Most cicadas rely on their camouflage to hide from predators and use flight to escape from them. A rather unusual escape behavior is known in the South African cicada *Nyara thanatotica*: When disturbed, it pretends to be dead, just as in some beetles.

Investigations of *Tibicen* species cicadas from North America reveal that some species are "warm-blooded," while others are "cold-blooded." In much the same way that moths vibrate their wings to raise the temperature of their flight muscles before they can fly, so some "warm-blooded" cicadas are able to use their muscles to warm up before they become active. The "cold-blooded" ones, however, have to wait until the warmth of the sun raises their body temperature before they can become active. The advantage of being able to raise the body temperature irrespective of the external temperature is that activity can be carried out even when it is cool, giving more time for feeding, courtship, and mating. However, cicadas are not truly warm-blooded in the way that birds and mammals are, since they maintain roughly the same body temperature night and day.

Making a Noise

Cicadas are among the noisiest of insects. The volume and strength of the sound produced by the males of some of the larger species is so great that it hurts the ears if a person comes too close. Even more surprisingly, if a large male cicada is picked up when he is calling, not only

do the ears hurt, but the vibrations passing through the fingers are almost painful. But not all cicadas are so noisy: Some of the smaller species produce calls that humans cannot hear because they are so high-pitched.

Dawn Chorus

Male cicadas begin to call just as the sun is coming up and the air temperature begins to rise. At first they produce a weak buzz; but as they warm up, it becomes a click, then a series of clicks with breaks in between, perhaps filled by a few buzzes. Finally, when they are warm enough, they will start their whole song. They do not break into full song right away because the muscles of the tymbal (the vibrating membrane) have to be warmed up first. Measurements taken in the wild of the tymbal muscle temperature of *Tibicen winnemanna* reveal the relationship between song and muscle temperature. The temperature rises gradually from roughly

⊕ *The dogday harvestfly,* Tibicen canicularis, *is found in woodlands in northeastern North America. Its call has been likened to that of a circular saw cutting a wooden board.*

How Sounds are Produced

The sound-producing organ is located beneath the front end of the male's abdomen. The way in which the sound-producing structure itself works is still not fully understood, despite it being first described as long ago as 1740. The part of the organ that actually produces the sound resembles a drum and is called the tymbal. Like a drum, it consists of a stiff membrane supported by a circular, rigid plate. Powerful muscles are attached to the membrane; when they contract and pull on it, a "click" is produced. The speed of producing the clicks and the amount of power put into them can be altered, and other structures within the organ can change the nature of the sounds that come out. Research on one North American cicada, *Tibicen winnemanna*, has thrown some light on the sequence of events taking place as a cicada calls. If the tymbal on one side is numbered 1 and the tymbal on the other side is 2, then the action sequence in the cicada is: In 1–In 2; Out 1–Out 2, where "In" denotes the muscle contracting to pull on the tymbal to make a click, and "Out" is the muscle relaxing and the tymbal clicking back to its resting position.

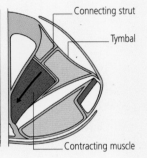

Cross sections of the cicada's sound-producing organs. On the left the muscle is relaxed, and the tymbal curves outward. On the right the muscle is contracted, the tymbal curve is reversed, and a "click" is produced.

Connecting strut

Tymbal

Contracting muscle

A Brevisiana species cicada feeds from a tree branch in Kenya. The proboscis, through which it is taking up sap from the tree, can be seen running from below its head down into the branch.

82 to 86°F (28 to 30°C) during the early buzzing period to around 97 to 104°F (36 to 40°C) during full song.

Male cicadas may emit a number of different sounds for use in different situations. *Fidicina mannifera* males from Central America, for example, produce four different types of sound. One type is only made when they are disturbed in some way, such as by an inquisitive bird. When the distance between the males is great, they overlap their song with those of other males; but when they are closer, they change to calling back and forth between one another. When individuals are close together, calls are often followed by a display in which they walk side by side, a behavior that has been interpreted as a way of determining which insect has the right to the particular calling site that they are perched on.

In a single habitat a number of species of male cicadas may be calling at the same time. Each has his own particular song, which is recognized by females of the same species. For example, in an area of rain forest in Veracruz State, Mexico, seven different species of cicada produced a raucous, mixed chorus as the sun rose and again as the sun set. Some males were found to sit alone and call; other species formed calling groups. Each species had its own particular height or site from which to sing. The females had to identify and locate the males of their own species from these habits.

The Cicada Life Cycle

In the majority of cicadas the purpose of the male's song is to attract females, although it can also bring together both males and females into the same area where they form mating pairs. Usually females travel to where the male is singing, but the role is occasionally reversed. In the Australian tick-tock cicada, *Cicadetta quadricincta*, the males move around in search of sitting females. The male still sings; but when he is close enough to a female, she responds by flicking her wings, making a sound that the male can hear and home in on. The more normal type of behavior takes place in species such as *Okanagana canadensis* and *O. rimosa* from North America. Males sit and sing from a suitable perch—cedars in the case of *O. canadensis* and broad-leaved vegetation for *O. rimosa*. Once the two sexes have found each other, they flick their wings at one another before mating.

Having mated, the female sets about laying her eggs. To do that, she cuts a slot with her ovipositor in a suitable twig and lays a batch of eggs into it. In some cases cutting into the twig causes it to die, and the twig eventually falls to the ground.

When fully developed, the nymphs escape from the eggshells and fall onto the ground if the twig their egg was laid into is still on the plant. The nymphs then use their enlarged digging front legs to burrow down into the soil until they reach the roots of their chosen food plant, where they begin to feed on its sap. Like other plant-sucking bugs, they produce large amounts of excess fluid from the anus, which they use to moisten the walls of the burrow. The fluid sticks the soil together, producing a smooth, long-lasting lining that allows them easy movement beneath the soil. All cicada nymphs are slow growing, spending a number of years beneath the soil. The longest time

⤒ Just a few species of cicada are found in the warmer regions of southern Europe. Here a pair of Cicada orni *are mating on the branch of a tree in the south of France.*

spent in the soil is in the periodical cicadas, which remain undergound for 17 years. As the time approaches for the nymph to molt to the adult form, it digs a burrow up to the soil surface, where in some species it may build a little mud chimney or turret around the top of the opening. The nymph climbs up the trunks or stems of surrounding vegetation and completes its molt to the adult form.

Like the dragonflies, the nymphs pass through a "teneral" stage lasting a few days during which they develop their full adult colors, and the skin hardens completely. From then on they are mature adults.

⊝ *In a rain forest in Queensland, Australia, a nymph of the cicada* Venustria superba *has just emerged from its final instar skin and is beginning to inflate its wings.*

Periodical Cicadas

Cicada nymphs feed by sucking sap from plant roots. The sap is very poor in food content. As a result, all cicadas, as far as is known, take at least two years to pass from newly hatched nymphs to the adult form. For most known cicada species adults are found every year, but in the periodical cicadas there are years in which no adults at all are present. The most well-known of the periodical cicadas are the species from North America, whose life cycles have been the subject of a great deal of research. These periodical cicadas belong to the genus *Magicicada,* and there are seven species. Four of them take 13 years to develop from egg to adult; the other three have a 17-year cycle. Amazingly, one of the 13-year species was first discovered as recently as the year 2000, not having previously been distinguished from similar species. Each species has what are known as "year classes," with each year class having a slightly different distribution within the eastern United States where they live. Because there may be some overlap between the year classes, periodical cicadas may appear more often than every 13 or 17 years.

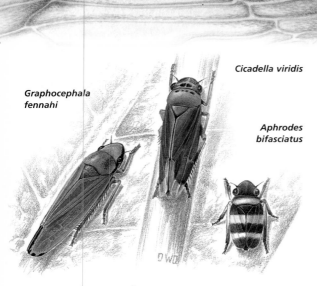

Cicadella viridis

Graphocephala fennahi

Aphrodes bifasciatus

DWD

Common name Leafhoppers

Family   Cicadellidae

Suborder   Auchenorrhyncha

Order   Hempitera

Number of species About 20,000 (2,500 U.S.)

Size   From about 0.08 in (2 mm) to 0.8 in (20 mm)

Key features Usually longer and slimmer than the spittlebugs they resemble, with an angular cross section to the tibiae; tibiae bear 1 or more rows of spines; forewings leathery, often brightly colored, distinguishing them from small cicadas

Habits   Usually found on their food plants; winged species will readily fly to escape when disturbed

Breeding   Many species stridulate to attract mates and during courtship, which may also involve "dance" routines; eggs laid in or on food plants

Diet   All species suck sap from plants, often living on just 1 particular plant species; like aphids, they produce honeydew

Habitat   Meadows, gardens, grassland, forests, marshes, mountains, and deserts

Distribution Worldwide, but more common in tropical zones

⤒ *The rhododendron leafhopper,* Graphocephala fennahi, *is found in the United States and Europe. Length 0.3–0.4 inches (8–10 mm).* Cicadella viridis *is from the Northern Hemisphere. Length 0.2–0.3 inches (6–8 mm).* Aphrodes bifasciatus *is the smallest of the three above and lives in Europe. Length 0.1–0.15 inches (3–4 mm).*

Leafhoppers   Cicadellidae

With 20,000 species the Cicadellidae is a large and varied family. Some leafhoppers take to the air to escape danger, while others perform "song and dance" routines to attract a mate or even to settle a dispute.

DISTINGUISHING LEAFHOPPERS FROM related families is not at all easy with the naked eye. However, with a good hand lens or microscope the differences are easy to see. The fully winged leafhoppers can be identified in the wild by their behavior: When disturbed, they jump and take flight to escape. By contrast, spittlebugs simply jump, and treehoppers usually rely on camouflage and are less likely to move.

Distinguishing Features

Viewed from above, leafhoppers have a triangular head, which sometimes has a projection such as a hornlike structure sticking out of the front. They tend to be longer and more slender than the other hoppers, and the forewings are often beautifully marked and colored in bright yellows, greens, and golds. There may also be some variations in color and markings within the same species, both

⤓ *Except for its unusual front legs, this* Peltocheirus *species leafhopper from the rain forest of Peru is typical of the family Cicadellidae.*

⤓ **Lissocarpa vespiformis,** *a South American rain-forest leafhopper, is a superb mimic of a small social wasp. The leafhopper, of course, has sucking mouthparts, while the wasp has chewing mouthparts.*

between different individuals and between the sexes. This is not true of all leafhoppers, however. Some species that have almost transparent forewings resemble tiny cicadas. In general, species that live high up in trees or bushes are fully winged, while those that live on or close to the ground are only partially winged. Under a microscope the main identifying feature for the family is the shape of the hind tibiae. Instead of being perfectly rounded, they have sharpish angles and one or more rows of small spines.

Feeding Habits and Pests

All leafhoppers feed by sucking fluid from plants. As with many other bug families there are those that use their stylets to cut into the

⊕ *Sitting on a leaf of Rhododendron ponticum in England are two rhododendron leafhoppers, Graphocephala fennahi. This insect can be a pest in its native North America, but it is the rhododendron that is the pest in England.*

phloem vessels of the plant, from which they are able to take up a solution rich in sugars and amino acids as well as other essential foods. There are also species that pierce the xylem, which contains mainly salts and water, and is very poor nutritionally. A few species feed very delicately by sucking out the sap from single cells one at a time.

Some bug species are restricted to feeding on just a single species of plant, while others may feed on a small range, often of closely related plants. Some leafhoppers are capable of feeding from many different plant species. With more than 20,000 species of leafhopper known to exist, and probably thousands more yet to be discovered, it is likely that almost every species of plant has at least one species of leafhopper using it as a source of food.

Because there are so many different species of leafhopper feeding on such a wide range of plants, it is logical that a fair number will infest cultivated crops and, as a result, will be pests. The damage they cause can be of two kinds: They can either harm the plant directly by feeding from it and robbing it of the food it needs to grow, or they can pass on viruses and other disease organisms as they feed. One example of a cicadellid that causes direct damage to the plant is the potato leafhopper, *Empoasca fabae*. It is not a pest of potatoes, as one might expect, but of alfalfa. Alfalfa is a member of the pea and bean family. In North America it is a very important crop and is grown in huge quantities to feed to livestock. It is so important that farmers actually prepare nesting sites for the bees that pollinate the plants. The potato leafhopper is a phloem feeder. Not only does it rob the plant of its food, but it also slows down the rate at which the plant can transport sugars and other substances from the leaves to the roots. That in turn slows down the growth of the plant.

The closely related *Empoasca vitis*, the vine leafhopper, is a pest in the grape-growing areas of Europe. The vine leaves turn brown; and if large numbers of the bug are present, the leaves can drop long before the fall, resulting in a serious reduction of the grape crop. The aster leafhopper, *Macrosteles quadrilineatus,* is a major carrier of a disease called the aster yellows. In both North and Central America it transmits the disease to crops such as carrots, lettuce, cabbage, and onions (among others), causing a great deal of damage. The disease is widespread around the world, where it is carried by other *Macrosteles* species or by other species of leafhopper.

A Lesson in Sharpshooting

An example of an insect that has become a pest as a result of human actions is illustrated by recent events in Oregon and Idaho. During the late 1990s foresters first began planting large numbers of poplar trees. Three years after the first planting it was noticed that there was considerable damage to the trees. Leaf buds were attacked, which stunted the trees' growth.

⊝ *These* Proconia marmorata *leafhoppers from Peru are all taking sap from a twig, reducing the amount of food available for the host plant and stunting its growth.*

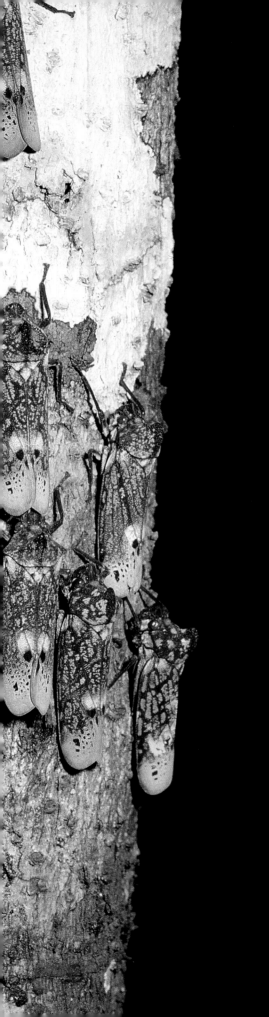

"Singing and Dancing"

Stridulation is common in leafhoppers, and the "songs" that are produced have different uses. What is known as the common song is used to tell other individuals of the same species that they are nearby. Courtship songs involve attracting males and females to one another, while pairing songs may be used during mating. The pairing song also doubles as a rivalry song when used by males of the same species.

A good example of a leafhopper "song and dance" routine is that of *Dalbulus* species males from Central America. The common song tells females that a male is nearby; once a female arrives, his song speeds up a little. The female then replies to his song with her own, and the duet brings the two into close proximity. Once they are close, the male begins his special courtship routine. He dances around the female in a rather jerky fashion, patting her every now and again with parts of his body. He sings at the same time, alternating the song with an occasional bout of wing buzzing, after which he may attempt to mate. If the female is ready for him, she will allow him to do so; otherwise she will warn him off with a good kick from her hind legs.

The female leafhoppers mate just once, so there is a great deal of rivalry between the males for a chance to mate. Rather than fighting each other (as occurs in some flies), two males in pursuit of the same female will approach each other and have a singing contest to decide which one will win. The rivalry song is used, and somehow—no one has yet been able to figure out just how—one male knows when he is beaten, and he will back off, leaving the winner to mate with the female. Once the female has mated, she normally lays her eggs into the stems of leaves on her chosen food plant.

The culprit was identified as *Graphocephala confluens*, the willow sharpshooter. The name sharpshooter describes the way in which the insects shoot off at high speed when disturbed, like a bullet from the gun of a sharpshooter.

The bug normally feeds on willow, but it is not a pest on that species because willows are not grown commercially in great numbers. Poplars are closely related to willows. The willow sharpshooters had discovered the new plantings of poplars, and switched their attentions to them. Because the trees occur in large numbers, the bugs thrived and have now reached pest proportions.

ⓓ *Leafhoppers of the same species can vary in color and markings, an example being the South American rain-forest species* **Rhaphirrhinus phosphoreus.**

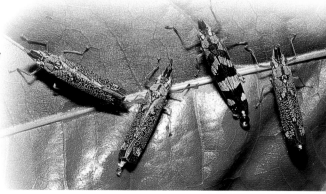

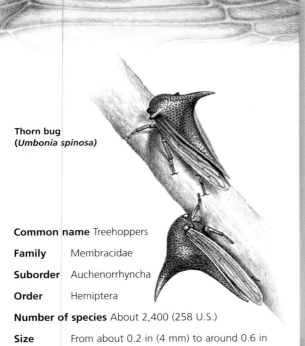

Thorn bug (*Umbonia spinosa*)

Common name Treehoppers

Family Membracidae

Suborder Auchenorrhyncha

Order Hemiptera

Number of species About 2,400 (258 U.S.)

Size From about 0.2 in (4 mm) to around 0.6 in (15 mm)

Key features Easily distinguished from the other small sap-sucking bugs by the pronotum, which extends back over the abdomen; pronotum may even extend beyond the end of the abdomen and can assume peculiar shapes, with spines and odd-shaped projections giving a bizarre appearance

Habits Often sit in large groups on their food plants; often camouflaged

Breeding Females of a few species indulge in parental care of eggs and nymphs

Diet Adults and nymphs are sap feeders, releasing honeydew as a by-product

Habitat Forests, grassland, and deserts

Distribution Worldwide, but concentrated in the tropics, especially those of the New World

⊕ *One species of thorn bug,* Umbonia spinosa, *is found in North and South America. The spiked shape and the green-and-red coloration both serve to deter predators. Length 0.4 inches (10 mm).*

Treehoppers Membracidae

The treehoppers include some very weird-looking species. A number of them do not look like insects at all, but more like a miniature alien from another planet.

THE FAMILY MEMBRACIDAE is found mainly in the tropics. Although commonly called treehoppers, by no means all species live on trees. For instance, the three-cornered alfalfa hopper, *Spissistilus festinus*, feeds on alfalfa crops, where it does considerable damage in its native southeastern United States.

Sap Feeders

Treehoppers are all sap feeders, and as a result, they produce honeydew. They keep the honeydew away from their body to prevent themselves getting gummed up with it. For that reason the rear end of the intestine forms what is called an "anal whip." That means the intestine can be pushed back to protrude a little way out of the rear end of the abdomen. The honeydew can be squirted out a short distance away from the bug's body, where it can do no harm to the insect. Nymphs of many species are visited by ants, which are very keen on honeydew as a food supplement.

As with the other hopper families, the treehoppers include a number of species that

⊕ *Although commonly known as thorn bugs, these* Umbonia spinosa *treehoppers from South America are probably not mimicking thorns at all. They are in fact quite visible, being warningly colored. It is more likely that the projections simply make them more difficult for predators to grasp and swallow.*

⊝ *The bizarre-shaped* Sphongophorus guerini *is from Trinidad, but odd-shaped species are also found in the Southwest of the United States, their shape almost certainly acting as a form of camouflage.*

The Pronotum

The feature that distinguishes the treehoppers from the other hopper families is the way in which the pronotum (the structure covering the top of the thorax) is developed. It can vary enormously from species to species and may form backward-pointing spikes or sideways-pointing horns. It may be large enough to cover the whole of the rest of the body, and it can even have the shape of another type of insect, such as an ant. A number of species resemble thorns and are called thorn bugs.

It is easy to understand why mimicking an ant or thorn is useful, but there seems no obvious explanation for the other weird pronotal shapes. One theory is that the peculiar shapes make it difficult for birds to grab hold of the bugs in their beaks. *Anolis* species lizards have been shown to be unable to grasp hold of treehoppers with long pronotal spines. However, if the thorn is cut off the pronotum, then the lizard has no problem in eating the bug. Outgrowths of the pronotum are not found in treehopper nymphs, but they may have spines or other outgrowths on the back or sides of the body.

are important pests either as a result of the direct damage they cause or because they transmit plant diseases.

The oakleaf hopper, *Platycotis vittata* from North America, is a pretty little insect with a horn sticking out of the front of the head. Unfortunately, severe infestations of the treehopper can cause discoloration of the leaves and dieback of the branches on economically important oak trees.

Helpful Hoppers

However, treehoppers can also be beneficial. The tropical plant genus *Lantana* originated in the Americas but has now spread throughout much of the world's tropics. It has become a pest in many areas, including the states of Queensland and New South Wales in Australia. Another North American treehopper, *Aconophora compressa*, has been introduced into Australia to help control the spread of the *Lantana* plants.

Treehoppers and Ants

Ants are well known scavengers, taking anything that is remotely edible back to the nest. They are particularly keen on honeydew, which is produced by many families of sap-sucking bugs, including the treehoppers. In most instances the ants visit the bugs and induce them to produce some honeydew by stroking them with their antennae. In return, the ants keep undesirable predatory insects and spiders away from the bugs. However, some relationships between treehoppers and ants are much more complicated.

Entylia species treehoppers live on members of the daisy family. One species, *E. bactriana* from North America, has been studied in detail. Females of the species remain with their egg masses until they hatch and then stay with them for the first two instars. Like *Umbonia* females, they protect their young from predators but not as actively. That role is given over to ants, which attend the treehoppers for a supply of honeydew. The treehopper has become so dependent on its protectors that no nymphs survive to adulthood in the wild unless the ants are present on the food plant. The nymphs remain together in groups to feed; any youngster that wanders off from the group puts itself at risk of attack, since the female is unable to keep watch over a wide area. The ants are able to keep the nymphs together by stroking them with their antennae as they take the honeydew. Keeping the nymphs together is also an advantage to the ant, since it can get a large supply of honeydew from a small area.

Scientists are eager to know whether the female treehoppers positively choose ant-covered plants on which to lay their eggs. Research on the North American treehopper *Publilia concava*, which lives on goldenrod, *Solidago altissima*, has thrown some light on the matter. The bugs are tended by *Formica* species ants. Scientists isolated a patch of plants that had neither ants nor bugs on them, but were close to the ants' nests. They then prevented the ants from visiting certain patches of the plants, but the treehoppers were allowed to get to the entire patch. The numbers of egg masses laid by the *P. concava* females over a period of weeks were then counted. It was found that almost twice the number of egg masses were laid on plants with ants on them than on plants without ants. It would seem, therefore, that the female treehoppers can tell whether the ants are present. They also seem to be able to tell that the ants are tending their offspring. If they are, the females are likely to desert them early and set about laying another batch of eggs. This is of advantage to both the bug and the ants—the bug has more offspring, and the ants get more honeydew.

Parental Care

Care of offspring by female treehoppers is not uncommon, especially in those species that live in the tropics. The thorn bug *Umbonia crassicornis* is a common insect in Central America and is also found in Florida. As a result of its availability, a great deal of research has been carried out on its lifestyle, particularly in relation to parental care. Although the bug is not typical of all members of the family Membracidae, many aspects of its life also occur in other species.

Like many treehoppers, the thorn bugs live on their food plant in large groups consisting of both adults and nymphs. Under normal circumstances they all sit with their heads facing toward the tip of the stem on which they live. The species is warningly colored, but males and females are easily distinguished from

⟳ *Antiantha expansa, a Mexican treehopper, is an example of adults and nymphs using different defenses. While the adults are green and look a bit like buds, the nymphs are bright red, an indication that they are probably unpleasant to eat.*

⟱ *Two ants of an unidentified species tend the females of the treehopper* Oxyrrhachis versicolor *on a plant in the Israeli desert. The bugs are guarding their eggs; the ants are getting honeydew as a reward for their protection.*

each other by the spike on the back of the pronotum. In females it has a sharp point, while in males the tip is flattened from side to side.

Riding on Her Back

Thorn bug males actively search for mates by walking around the food plant, and both sexes fan their wings in what is thought to be a pheromone-spreading action. Males attracted to a female will follow her around, sometimes for several days. At times a male may climb onto her back and be carried around for a few days. Such long, drawn-out riding behavior seems to be a necessary part of courtship in tropical treehoppers and has been noted as occurring in other species. Eventually, the riding male is allowed to mate with the female. He climbs off her back, turns so that they are tail to tail, and then the sex organs are brought together as they mate. The mating process is much shorter than the courtship and lasts 45 minutes to just under an hour.

Egg Laying

When she is ready to lay her eggs, the female uses her ovipositor to insert them under the bark of a soft, relatively young twig of her chosen food plant. In Florida that is usually a *Calliandra* species "powderpuff" of the pea and bean family (Fabaceae). Having laid her eggs, the female then sits quietly, fairly close to them. She shows little or no response to any kind of disturbance until about five days before the eggs are due to hatch, when she becomes more active. At that time, if another treehopper or any threatening creature such as an ant or spider comes near, the female buzzes her wings at them to warn them off.

Shortly before the eggs are due to hatch out, the female moves up toward the bud at the tip of the twig and, using her ovipositor, cuts a slit in the twig surface about 0.2 inches

(5 mm) long. She then cuts similar slits to create a spiral of them around the twig, the whole process taking anything from one to two hours. On hatching, the nymphs stay on the remains of the egg mass for up to 12 hours but then move to the area of slits that have been cut by their mother, where they feed. The mother stays with them for several instars. She buzzes her wings to drive off any predators that try to take her nymphs. She will also attempt to herd any offspring that wander off back into the safety of the main group.

The female's role in guarding her young is quite important, since unguarded nymphs do not last very long, ending up as prey for a variety of insects and spiders. If a nymph in a guarded group is injured by a predator, it releases alarm pheromones that instruct the mother to fight off the attacker.

Guarding of the young by the mother is quite a common occurrence in the Membracidae, and the production of alarm pheromones has also been recorded for other treehopper species.

⊕ **Hepteronotus reticulatus** *is a rain-forest treehopper from Central America. Its pronotum extends backward, mimicking an ant with open jaws. It gains protection from the fact that most predators keep well away from ants because they bite.*

① *The treehopper* Enchonopa
concolor *from the tropical savannas of
the* campo cerrado *region of Brazil is probably
a true thorn mimic. Not only does it look like a thorn,
but it lives on a thorny* Solanum *species host plant.*

Parental Care in Aetalionid Treehoppers

Close relations of the Membracidae, and sometimes included with them, are the treehoppers of the family Aetalionidae (or Aethalionidae). These prettily marked bugs resemble the Membracidae but do not have the highly modified pronotum. They are found in the tropical regions of the New World.

The females of some species are subsocial in that they spend some time caring for their eggs in the company of other females of the same species. They lay batches of around 100 eggs in a sticky mass, which then hardens, on the stem of their host plant. They then sit head down on top of the pile of eggs, sweeping their legs along the sides from time to time to disturb any parasitic wasps that may be trying to lay their eggs inside the bug eggs. The leg-sweeping action eventually gives the egg mass a rather polished appearance. The protection afforded the eggs is not perfect, since in order to feed, the females have to tip forward over the front of the mass, leaving the rear exposed to the wasps.

When the eggs hatch, the nymphs remain close to one another and the other colony members so that there can finally be masses of adults and nymphs of all sizes. As is so often the case with sap-feeding bugs, they are tended by various species of ants for their honeydew; the ants providing them with protection in return.

Females of the net-winged twighopper, Aetalion reticulatum, *guard their egg sacs in the Brazilian rain forest. They are also being protected by ants in return for their honeydew.*

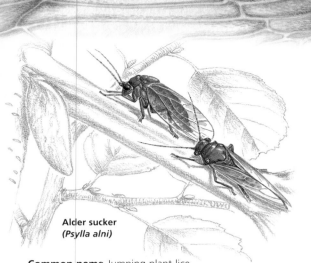

Alder sucker
(Psylla alni)

Common name Jumping plant lice

Family Psyllidae

Suborder Sternorrhyncha

Order Hemiptera

Number of species About 1,300 (257 U.S.)

Size From about 0.05 in (1.5 mm) to 0.2 in (5 mm)

Key features Resemble tiny cicadas, but forewings more leathery than hind wings; wings held like a tent over the body while at rest; hind legs well developed for jumping, but flight is rather weak; nymphs are rather odd looking, having flattened, circular, or oval bodies with the wing buds sticking out to the sides; nymphs produce waxy secretions that cover and protect them

Habits Adults sit on their food plants, often in fairly large numbers, taking to the air when disturbed; some species make galls

Breeding Both sexes, at least of some species, use sounds during courtship and mating; eggs laid on the food plant

Diet All species suck sap from their host plants; a number of species are pests of cultivated trees

Habitat Most species live on trees and tend to be forest dwellers

Distribution Worldwide

⬆ *The tiny alder sucker,* Psylla alni, *ranges across the Northern Hemisphere wherever its favorite alder trees are found. Length 0.05–0.1 inches (1.5–3.5 mm).*

 SEE ALSO Cicadas 24:80; Aphids 24:100

Jumping Plant Lice

Psyllidae

With many species able to produce several generations a year it is no wonder that the tiny jumping plant lice can become pests on trees.

BOTH SEXES OF ADULTS of the family Psyllidae are similar in appearance, although in some species the males may be smaller than the females. In the many species whose adults have a relatively long life (meaning months rather than weeks), there can be a distinctive change in overall color as they age. Starting off green when they first emerge as adults, they gradually change color through red to brown and finally black.

Both adults and nymphs of the Psyllidae are phloem feeders (feeding on tissues of the vascular system of plants), and they produce large amounts of honeydew. While nymphs are always found on their associated food plants, adults may be found away from them, especially where the winters are cold, when they use conifers as shelter.

⊙ *Adults and nymphs of the alder sucker,* Psylla alni, *on a leaf of their host tree,* Alnus glutinosa, *beside an English river. The nymphs have a covering of floury wax, while the adults resemble tiny cicadas.*

Protective Wax

The nymphs produce powdery wax or strings of wax from special glands. In gall-forming species, where the nymphs are enclosed, the wax is used to cover liquid waste products so that the colony is not contaminated. Nymphs of some species—especially those of the subfamily Spondyliaspinae from Australia—produce honeydew but do not get rid of it immediately. They hold it on the end of the abdomen until enough water has evaporated from it, and sticky pellets of sugar are

formed. They then use the pellets to make protective shelters called "lerps." Lerps are like tents but are more usually shaped like a mussel shell. Each different species has its own particular shape of lerp, which is a good aid to their identification. With their high sugar content, lerps are a favorite with some birds.

Birds are not alone in making use of lerps: In Iran they have been collected for centuries by humans in order to make a kind of sweetmeat called "gaz" or "gazz."

Varied Life Cycles

In species with the simplest life cycles the first instar nymphs hatch from overwintered eggs that have been laid on the host plant. They then pass through five nymphal stages before becoming adult. Some species may produce further generations until late summer, when the females lay their overwintering eggs on the host plant. These adults then die, but those of some species may overwinter to breed again in the following spring.

The pear psylla, *Cacophylla pyri,* is a species with overwintering adults. It is an important pest that causes a great deal of damage in pear orchards in its native Europe and in other countries where it has been accidentally introduced. The overwintering adults arise from the last generation of nymphs and emerge gradually during the winter months. Research in the south of France has revealed that the first of the winter forms appears in early September, and adults continue to emerge until January or sometimes later. The female ovaries develop slowly during the winter months, but females never mate with any of the previous generation of summer males, even if the females emerge in the fall when the males are still present.

In the tropics temperature is less of a problem, and psyllids may pass through many generations each year. The Asiatic or oriental citrus psyllid, *Diaphorina citri,* is a pest of citrus fruits both in Asia and in Florida, where it was first noted in 1998. In its new home it can produce nine or 10 generations each year.

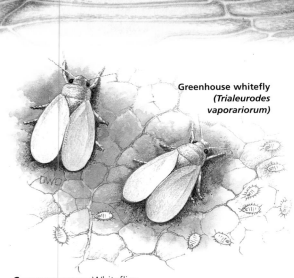

Greenhouse whitefly
(*Trialeurodes
vaporariorum*)

Common name Whiteflies

Family Aleyrodidae

Suborder Sternorrhyncha

Order Hemiptera

Number of species About 1,160 (100 U.S.)

Size Up to 0.1 in (2–2.5 mm)

Key features Tiny insects covered in a waxy powder that gives them a white appearance; membranous wings, which are white or mottled, held almost flat over the body, with slight overlap along the centerline; early nymphs have legs and can move around, later instars cannot use legs and remain in one place

Habits Often found in large numbers on food plants; nymphs cover the underside of leaves; adults fly readily with a weak flight when disturbed

Breeding Reproduction is sexual or by parthenogenesis; when courtship occurs, it can be complex; eggs laid singly or in batches; parental care has been recorded

Diet All species suck sap from host plants; a number are pests of cultivated plants

Habitat Forests, fields, plantations, and orchards

Distribution Worldwide, but more species in the warmer regions

⊕ *The greenhouse whitefly,* Trialeurodes vaporariorum, *is a worldwide pest of tomatoes and houseplants. As well as sucking nutrients from the plants, the sugary honeydew excreted gets infested with fungi. Length 0.1 inches (2 mm).*

Whiteflies Aleyrodidae

Whiteflies resemble tiny white moths. They can exist in very large numbers, flying off from greenhouse plants and forming "clouds" when they are disturbed.

THE WHITE APPEARANCE OF members of the family Aleyrodidae is due to the presence of a white coating of waxy dust over the whole insect. The two pairs of paddle-shaped, transparent wings extend well beyond the end of the body.

Both male and female adults are fully winged, but males tend to be smaller than females. Although they appear to be rather weak in flight, they can cover considerable distances. Using a wind tunnel, researchers found that the sweet potato whitefly, *Bemesia tabaci*, found throughout the tropics, was able to remain in flight for up to two hours at a time. Individuals marked with a fluorescent dust and released into the wild were recovered nearly 1.4 miles (2 km) away. That helps explain the rapid spread of some pest species when accidentally introduced into new regions.

Apart from transmitting virus diseases of crop and ornamental plants, the bugs themselves can cause considerable damage. Both adults and feeding nymphal stages produce large quantities of honeydew, which coats their food plants. The honeydew becomes infected with various fungi, giving the plant a

⊕ *Underneath this mass of waxy filaments are the nymphs of an unidentified Australian rain-forest whitefly. The disguise will fool most predators.*

The greenhouse whitefly, Trialeurodes vaporariorum, *is a pest on many greenhouse crops worldwide. Here masses of them are feeding on tomato leaves, stunting the growth of the plant and reducing the crop of fruit as a result.*

sooty appearance. That impairs photosynthesis and therefore the plant's growth.

Rough Courtship

Males of the worldwide greenhouse pest *Trialeurodes vaporariorum* seek out females by making contact with any individual—male or female—with their antennae and front legs. If it turns out to be an interested female, the male begins his courtship. First, he moves alongside her and with one antenna taps on her thorax; with the other he taps the underside of her antennae. As he does so, he begins to flutter his wings. He then stops fluttering, vibrates the antenna that is farthest away from his mate, and then bumps her on the thorax with his head and front legs. At the same time, he fans his wings and taps her with his antennae. The two latter activities can be repeated up to 25 times until the female allows him to mate.

Females lay their egg batches beneath a leaf of the food plant. The number of eggs varies between species and individuals—the highest number recorded being 300 by a sweet potato whitefly. The eggs are normally laid in a series of circles or curves. The female carries out the process while feeding, rotating her body around her rostrum, which is embedded in the plant. Some whiteflies, however, lay single eggs here and there on the leaf. The female inserts the egg into the surface of the leaf on the end of a hollow stalk called the pedicel. The stalk allows the egg to take in water from the leaf while the first instar nymph is developing inside.

There are five instars, the first of which—called a "crawler"—has antennae and legs, and is able to move short distances. All of the following instars lack working legs. Their legs are just short stumps, although they are a little longer in the fourth instar, which remains fixed in one place as it feeds through the rostrum. The fifth instar does not feed and is similar to the pupal stage of higher insects, such as butterflies. Adult structures form inside the fifth instar, which finally molts as a fully developed male or female whitefly.

**Peach-potato aphid
(Myzus persicae)**

Common name Aphids

Family Aphididae

Suborder Sternorrhyncha

Order Hemiptera

Number of species About 3,800 (1,380 U.S.)

Size From about 0.04 in (1 mm) to 0.2 in (5 mm)

Key features Most commonly green or pink in color, but may be brown or black; females normally wingless; in males both pairs of wings transparent and folded tentlike over the body; body rather soft; abdomen with pair of cornicles on fifth or sixth abdominal segment

Habits Adults and nymphs usually found together in huge numbers on their host plants, on above-ground structures, or on plant roots

Breeding Life cycles can be very complex, including parthenogenesis and alternating of host plant species

Diet All suck the sap of plants, producing honeydew as a by-product; some species produce and live in galls

Habitat Forests, meadows, grassland, moorland, on waterside and floating plants, marshes, and seashore

Distribution Worldwide, but with the greater number of species in temperate regions

⊕ *Found all over the world, the very common peach-potato aphid, Myzus persicae, feeds on more than 200 plants, including peaches and potatoes, on which it is a pest. As a carrier of the fungal disease potato blight, this species helped cause the Irish potato famine in the 1840s, which was responsible for the deaths of almost 1 million people. Length 0.07 inches (2 mm).*

Aphids

Aphididae

With their complicated life cycles, various physical forms, and fascinating methods of defense the aphids include some of the most interesting and unusual of insect species.

THE 3,800 SPECIES INCLUDED within the Aphididae are composed of a number of subfamilies, which some scientists consider to be families in their own right. Therefore, classification of the group can be quite messy. It is not at all easy to define a typical aphid. Their appearance may depend on the species, which food plant they appear on, and the time of year.

Perhaps the most obvious feature of an aphid is the pair of cornicles, which produce wax and pheromones for defense purposes. The cornicles are a pair of tubes that stick up from the upper side of the fifth, or sometimes the sixth, abdominal segment. In a few species of aphid, however, the cornicles appear as rings on the surface of the abdomen or may be missing altogether.

Sugar Manufacturers

Aphids feed by inserting their rostrum into the phloem tubes of their host plants. The phloem is a tissue in the plant that is used for transportation of the products of photosynthesis. As a result, it is rich in nutrients, and the aphids grow quite rapidly. They take in more sugars and water than they need and as a consequence produce large quantities of honeydew. So much honeydew may be produced that, standing beneath a tree that is heavily infested with aphids, it can seem as if it is drizzling with rain. A few aphids are restricted to a single food plant or to one or two closely related species. Many change their food plants as the season goes alongs. The number of alternate plant species that they are capable of feeding on varies between species.

⊕ *Brachycaudus cardui from Europe lives on various thistle plants. In the group seen here the black individuals have been parasitized by a wasp and will die. The brown specimens are already dead, while the green ones are healthy.*

The most commonly seen aphids are those that rely on different species of plants at different times of the year. As a result, there are different generations of the aphid on different plants. However, things are not always so simple. A number of aphid species may alternate between three different hosts at different times of the season, and the number of plant hosts on which a single generation lives can also vary considerably.

An Aphid's Life

The bean aphid, *Aphis fabae*, which occurs in much of North America and Europe, is a good example of such host switching. At the end of the winter the bean aphid (along with many other species) exists only as eggs that have spent the harshest months of the year attached to a woody host plant. As temperatures rise in the spring, sap begins to rise in these plants, and the aphid eggs hatch. From them emerge only wingless females, which feed on the sap.

The females are able to produce offspring—all wingless females—without having mated, a phenomenon known as parthenogenesis. Further generations of wingless females may then appear, again by parthenogenesis, until the sap in the host plant becomes less nutritious. That is the signal for the wingless females to produce a generation of winged

⊕ *Aphids mating. Reproduction without mating—known as parthenogenesis—is common in aphids.*

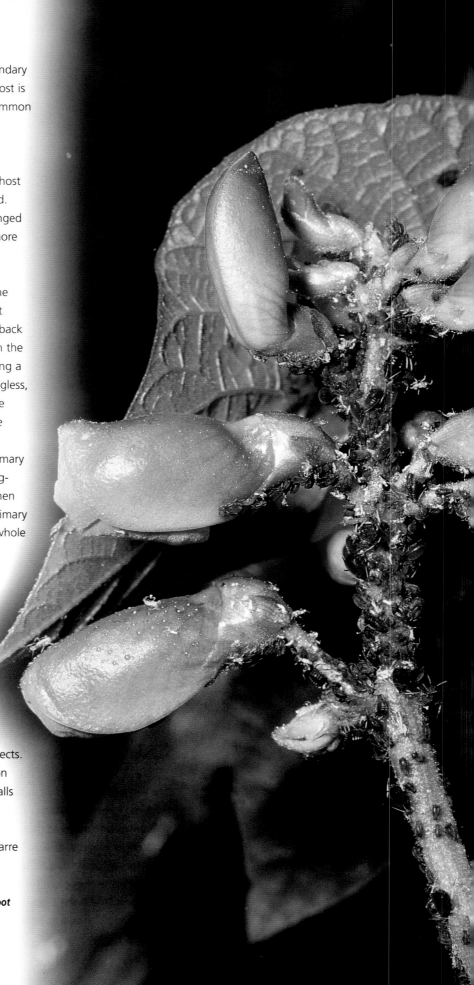

females, which then fly off to seek a secondary host. In the case of *A. fabae* a common host is field or broad beans, giving them their common name. On the new host plant the winged females produce a generation of wingless females. They in turn produce further generations of wingless females until the host plant begins to run out of supplies of food. Once again, this is the signal for more winged females to appear, which then fly on to more secondary host plants where the whole fascinating cycle continues.

As the end of summer approaches, the females on the secondary host plants start giving birth to winged females, which fly back to the woody primary host plants. In them the sap is now flowing well again and providing a good supply of food. A generation of wingless, egg-producing females is now born. In the meantime those females remaining on the secondary host plants are giving birth to winged males, which fly to the woody primary host plants, where they mate with the egg-producing females. Each of the females then lays four to six eggs on the bark of the primary host. The eggs then overwinter, and the whole cycle is repeated the following year.

Root Feeders and Gall Formers

Some aphids are seldom encountered, since they feed on the roots of their host plants, or they form plant galls. The colony remains mostly hidden inside the gall. The European cherry aphid, *Myzus cerasi*, for example, feeds from the underside of cherry leaves, causing the leaves to roll up and form a protective chamber around the insects. *Eriosoma* species, which are widespread on elms in the Northern Hemisphere, form galls by rolling the leaves of the host plants.

Eriosoma yangi, a Japanese species, however, goes about things in a more bizarre

⊝ **Adults and nymphs of the bean aphid, Aphis fabae, *feed in large numbers on the flowering shoot of a string bean plant.***

way. Individual females feed on young elm leaves until they molt into the third instar. The *E. yangi* nymph is apparently unable to induce galls by itself and so seeks out those created by other *Eriosoma* species aphids. The *E. yangi* nymph enters the gall, kills its real owner, and takes possession of the gall. Occasionally the original owner is not killed, and the two different species live together in the gall, feeding and producing live young, which remain clustered around their own mother.

"Superglue"

Being tiny and very soft-bodied, aphids have many enemies. At first glance they appear to have no defenses. This, however, is not the case. Birds do not normally feed on aphids unless they are very hungry, since aphids are not a particularly rich source of food for large animals. They do, however, provide an acceptable meal for other insects, including ladybugs and their larvae, lacewing larvae, and the larvae of a number of hover fly species. Another group of enemies is the parasitic wasps—tiny wasps that lay their egg onto an aphid, which then itself becomes the food for their larva to live on. Examination of any aphid colony will usually reveal the fruit of the parasitic wasps' labors: rather bloated, motionless aphids, normally an unusual color, which are slowly being devoured from the inside by the wasp larva.

The aphids defend themselves against such unwanted attentions by using the two cornicles on the abdomen. When the aphid is disturbed, perhaps by a tiny parasitic wasp landing on it,

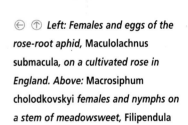

⬅ ⬆ *Left: Females and eggs of the rose-root aphid,* Maculolachnus submacula, *on a cultivated rose in England. Above:* Macrosiphum cholodkovskyi *females and nymphs on a stem of meadowsweet,* Filipendula ulmaria, *in an English hedgerow. The female at the top left is giving birth to a young one parthenogenetically.*

the bug secretes a tiny drop of a waxy substance from each cornicle. It is a bit like superglue, since when the wax comes into contact with any part of the wasp, it immediately sets solid, gluing the attacker to its victim. As a result, both the aphid and its attacker will eventually die.

Such a strategy might seem like suicide for the aphid; but since nearly all the aphids in a group are sisters, one sacrificing her life is worthwhile for the group as a whole. A single parasitic wasp, hover fly larva, or ladybug could kill a much larger number of aphids if allowed to go free. Alarm pheromones are also secreted by the cornicles, which spread through the colony, warning other aphids that they are in danger of attack.

Soldier Aphids

Although the presence of soldier castes in ants and termites has been known for more than 200 years, it is only as recently as 1977 that some aphids were also found to have a soldier caste. Since then research has indicated that soldiers have appeared independently at least four times in different lines of aphid. The first report was of soldiers of the woolly aphid, *Colophina clematis*, from Japan. The soldiers, which are sterile first instar nymphs, attack predatory insects and their eggs by jabbing at them with their sharp stylets. They have also been observed to attack aphids of different species living on the same plant, perhaps in an attempt to reduce competition for space.

Other species of aphids produce soldiers complete with structural modifications for the job. An Asian bamboo-feeding species, *Pseudoregma alexanderi*, has first instar soldiers that resemble pseudoscorpions. Each soldier has enlarged grasping front legs and a pair of sharp horns on the front of the head. Predators, such as lacewing larvae, are attacked by groups of soldiers, which pierce them with their horns. The result is that the larva is either completely immobilized where it stands or falls to the ground with the soldiers still attached to it.

Investigations in Europe into the activities of the soldiers of *Pemphigus spyrothecae*, which make galls on the leaf stalks of the black poplar, *Populus nigra*, revealed that they were able to chase off ladybug larvae, young hover fly larvae, and the early instars of the flower bug, *Anthocoris nemoralis*. The aphids always lose a few soldiers in the attack. But considering that a flower bug nymph can kill off the whole aphid colony, the loss of a few soldiers is worth the sacrifice.

Sugar Cravings

Ants are known to "milk" aphids for their honeydew. There is some evidence to indicate

⬅ *A ladybug beetle adult (Coccinellidae) feeds on an aphid in Transvaal, South Africa. Ladybugs and their larvae are important predators of aphids.*

Aphid Pests

Aphids include some of the worst pests of human crops in the temperate zones of the world. The list of pest aphids is long, and the list of plant species attacked almost endless. The bean aphid, *Aphis fabae*, for example, uses as secondary hosts not just members of the pea and bean family but also a variety of cultivated ornamental plants as well. A number of different species of aphid attack cereals such as wheat and barley wherever they are grown. Today the only way to control their numbers is by using insecticides.

In the United States rosy apple aphids, *Dysaphis plantaginea*, are a major pest of fruit orchards. They cause the apple tree leaves to curl up and the fruit to become misshapen and to ripen before it is fully developed. The green apple aphid, *Aphis pomi*, which was probably introduced into North America when settlers imported the first apple trees from Europe, is also a widespread orchard pest, damaging the soft young growth of apple trees and their ability to produce fruit.

Aphid pests continue to spread as people introduce new crops in new areas. Soybean has been an important crop in North America for some time, but it was only in 2000 that one of its major pests, the soybean aphid, *Aphis glycines*, a native of China, Japan, and Southeast Asia, was first discovered here. It was so widespread and present in such numbers on the soybean that it had obviously arrived some years previously and had become established without being noticed. How far it will spread in its new habitat and how damaging it will be in the long run is yet to be learned. Sadly, over recent years the aphid has also made its way into Australia, where soybean is now grown in some quantities.

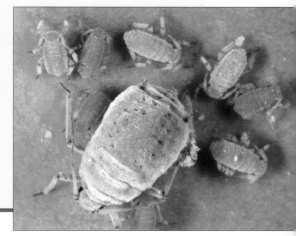

that the ants are in fact attracted to the sugar in the honeydew. Investigation of three *Chaitophorus* aphid species from Europe revealed that two of the three species produced honeydew containing the sugar melezitose, much favored by ants. The two sugar producers are regularly visited by ants, but the nonproducer is not.

⬆ *A cabbage aphid female,* Brevicoryne brassicae, *and the offspring that she has produced by parthenogenesis, pictured in California.*

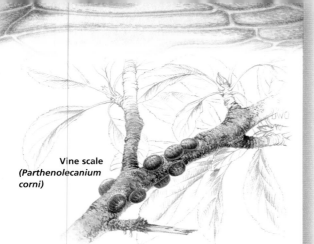

**Vine scale
(Parthenolecanium
corni)**

Common name	Scale insects (soft, wax, and tortoise scales)
Family	Coccidae
Suborder	Sternorrhyncha
Order	Hemiptera
Number of species	About 1,000 (84 U.S.)
Size	From about 0.04 in (1 mm) to 0.2 in (5 mm)
Key features	Males and females look completely different; males lack mouthparts and have just 1 front pair of transparent, membranous wings, the 2nd pair resembling the halteres of the flies; alternatively, males may be wingless but still recognizable as insects; females may not resemble normal insects: the rostrum is present, but antennae are tiny or nonexistent; normal division of the body into segments not clear; top of the body is covered by a plate resembling a fish scale; wings absent; legs reduced and often nonworking; a powdery or waxy coating may also be present on the body
Habits	Females most often found fixed in one place to any part of their host plant or plants, usually in quite large numbers
Breeding	Females cannot fly and are sought out by the males; life cycles are quite complicated
Diet	Females are sap feeders, often on a single plant species, and produce honeydew as a by-product
Habitat	Grassland, forests, gardens, orchards, fields, and deserts
Distribution	Worldwide, but more species are found in tropical regions

⊕ *The vine scale, Parthenolecanium corni, is a widespread plant pest. It damages the leaves and fruit of the plants it lives on due to the growth of a sooty mold on the honeydew produced by the bug. Length 0.2 inches (6 mm).*

Scale Insects

Coccidae

Originally from Africa and the Americas, the family Coccidae is now found worldwide—a result of their host plants having been transported around the globe.

IT IS HARD TO TELL FROM appearances that some members of the family Coccidae are insects at all. However, it is fairly easy to recognize the males as insects, since they are very similar to mealybug males. They are tiny and either have just the forewings developed for flying—with the hind wings forming halteres, like those of flies—or they are wingless. Unlike most insects, which have very complicated arrangements of veins on the wings, male scale insects have only a couple of veins to support each wing. The division of the body into a separate head, thorax, and abdomen can be seen clearly.

That is not the case, however, with the females. In most species of scale insects the females have reduced legs and limited mobility until they become full of eggs. The thorax and abdomen are fused together as a single unit, and it is impossible to see any clear form of segmentation. The arrangement at the rear end of the abdomen is unusual and is the best way to identify a female scale insect. The end of the abdomen extends back on either side of the anus and forms a cleft.

Scaly Females

Not all female members of the family produce scales; but where scales are present, they are the result of a thickening of the upper surface of the body. The scales are often shiny brown and resemble fish scales. Alternatively, they can be very similar to one half of the shell of a bivalve mollusk, such as a clam. Various amounts of shiny or powdery wax may also cover the female's body.

Scale insects are most often found on twigs or positioned along the midribs and veins of leaves, where they feed from the plant sap. They also form associations with ants, which collect honeydew produced by the bugs. Some species are known to associate with ants inside ant plants. Ants build their nests inside these hollow plants. The plant benefits by receiving nitrates from the ants' droppings as they decompose. Some scale insects have also taken advantage of the shelter and food provided by the ant plants as well as the protection they receive from the ants that live there.

Another recently discovered scale insect has a relationship with a stingless bee species of the genus *Schwarzula*. The bees build their nests in tree branches, in tunnels burrowed out by moth

⊙ **Pulvinaria regalis** *is a widespread species of scale insect that occurs on a large range of trees. An adult female feeds on one of its favorite host plants, a bay tree.*

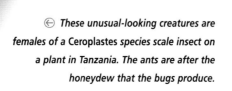

⊙ *These unusual-looking creatures are females of a* Ceroplastes *species scale insect on a plant in Tanzania. The ants are after the honeydew that the bugs produce.*

⊙ *The soft scale,* Coccus hesperidium, *is a widespread pest of ornamental plants in greenhouses. The large female is in the company of some smaller nymphs.*

↑ A dense infestation of an unidentified scale insect on a plant in savanna in Kenya. The Dolichoderus species ants are collecting honeydew.

↑ *Unidentified scale insects, attended by ants, feed on grass leaves in Kenya. It is just possible to see the insect segmentation through the semitransparent exoskeleton.*

caterpillars. The bees collect the honeydew and wax produced by the scale insects that live in the tunnels alongside them. The bees use the honeydew as food and build their nests with the wax.

As in other families within the Sternorrhyncha, scale insects may reproduce sexually or parthenogenetically, or both,

depending on species. *Parthenolecanium corni*, the brown scale, for example, has strains that are sexual and some that are parthenogenetic.

Males either fly or walk to find a female with which to mate. Once mated, the females produce their eggs. The eggs are usually given some form of protection, which varies from one genus to another. In some females the soft parts of the body shrivel up inside the exoskeleton, leaving a chamber in which the eggs develop. In *Physokermes* females the chamber can contain up to 3,000 eggs.

Ovisacs and Brood Pouches

An alternative form of protection is for the female to manufacture an ovisac out of threads of wax, which she places either below or

⤓ *Pads of an opuntia cactus, infested with nymphs of the cochineal bug, Dactylopius coccus. These plants are growing in the Canary Islands, thousands of miles from the bug's original home in Mexico.*

behind her body. Females of some genera retain the eggs as they develop inside a special brood pouch, which forms in the region near the reproductive opening from the abdomen. The first instar nymphs hatch inside this pouch and may remain there for a while before eventually emerging into the outside world.

Females of most species of scale insect have just two instars before becoming adult, although a few have three. The males have only two instars, the second one forming a pupa similar to that of the higher insects such as flies in the Diptera. Both male and female nymphs, known as "crawlers," have legs and are mobile. It is almost certainly during the nymphal stages that the insects disperse from one plant to the next. They are very tiny in the early instars, and it is quite possible for them to be blown by the wind to a new plant.

Cochineal Bugs

Cochineal bugs, or cochineal insects, in the family Dactylopiidae are relatives of the scale insects. As their common name suggests, they are best known for producing the pigment cochineal, which for years was the main dye used to color foods all shades from pink to deep red. Although it has recently fallen from popularity, scares about the possible cancer-producing properties of modern synthetic dyes may mean that cochineal will come back into common use again. It is still used in Mexico as a fabric dye.

It is believed that the cochineal—which has a very bitter taste—is a defense against attacks from ants. However, the dye does not stop caterpillars of the moth *Laetilia coccidivora* from preying on the insect. Amazingly, the moth caterpillar retains the cochineal in its body, where it acts as a defense against its own ant enemies.

Dactylopius species cochineal bugs live on opuntia cacti. A number of large opuntias have been introduced from the Americas to other parts of the world as ornamental plants. Some of the introduced cacti have managed to become established in the wild, where they have become a problem. Introduction of *Dactylopius* cochineal bugs from their native America has, in most cases, brought the pest opuntias rapidly under control.

Male Pupae

The way in which pupation occurs in male scale insects is very unusual. The exoskeleton becomes broken up into just a few large, glassy plates to form a chamber called the puparium. Inside the chamber the second instar nymph molts to become a prepupa, which then forms the pupa. Development to the adult male stage takes place inside the pupa. When the male is ready to emerge, he backs out through a hinge in the rear plate of the puparium. As the male moves backward, the hinge lifts up, allowing him to escape.

Wide-Ranging Pests

Many of the known species of scale insects are pests to some degree, since they are found on a wide variety of plant species—a number of them grown by humans. The feeding scale insects adversely affect their food plants, reducing the length of the side branches so that the overall growth of the plant is slower than usual. Some species have a very wide range of host plants. The brown scale, *Parthenolecanium corni*, can live on hazel, peach, plum, ash, and lime trees, as well as various currant, blackberry, and rose bushes, grapevines, and broom. It is a pest of cultivated hazels (which provide cobnuts), as well as fruit trees.

Woolly Insects

Pulvinaria vitis (sometimes called the woolly vine scale, cottony vine scale, or woolly currant scale) is another species, originally from Europe, that has now made its way to most temperate parts of the world. It is a pest of grapes and various currants. The list of plants on which it can live is almost endless and includes peach, apricot, gooseberry, sour cherry, and a whole range of trees and shrubs. The common name woolly vine scale comes from the ovisac, which is like cotton wool. It can grow so big that it pushes the whole body of the female away from the plant stem. Since she does not withdraw her stylets while she is feeding from the stem, she slowly heads toward the vertical, the stylets acting as a kind of hinge between the stem and her body.

Originally thought to be from southern Africa, the soft brown scale, *Coccus hesperidum*, has also found its way to most parts of the world, where it has become a major pest of citrus fruit trees. It is now kept under reasonable control by a number of different parasitic wasps and beetles that either use it as a host or feed on the crawlers. Yet it is still quite common on various indoor plants, where its honeydew causes the leaves to be covered with a sticky coating. Eventually, the leaves can become black with mold as a result of the damage caused by the honeydew.

⊖ *A group of unidentified female scale insects on a plant in the campo cerrado region of Brazil. Each female has produced a large mass of eggs.*

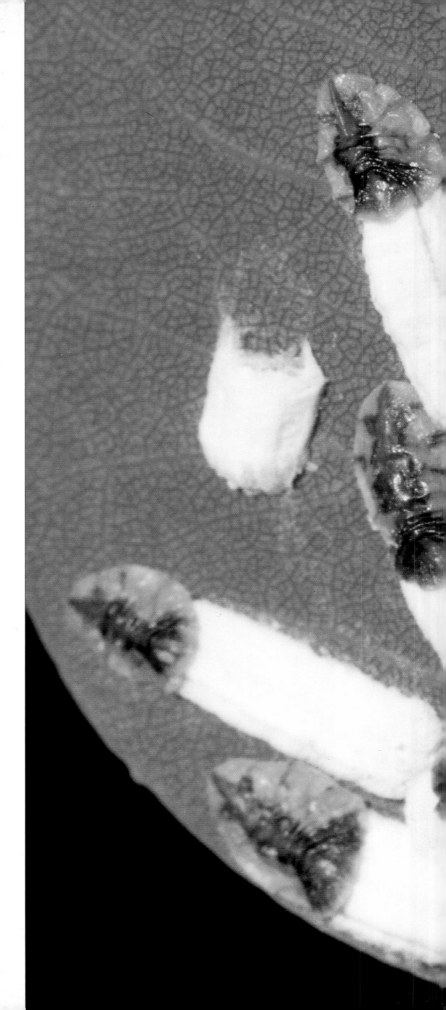

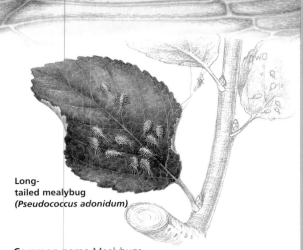

Long-
tailed mealybug
(*Pseudococcus adonidum*)

Common name Mealybugs

Family Pseudococcidae

Suborder Sternorrhyncha

Order Hemiptera

Number of species About 1,100 (60 U.S.)

Size From around 0.04 in (1 mm) to 0.2 in (5 mm)

Key features Oval-shaped insects with distinct body segments; females wingless; males with a single pair of forewings or wingless; separation of the body into head, thorax, and abdomen not clearly visible in females, but head is obvious in males; males lack compound eyes, but ommatidia are present; whole body covered in a powdery wax coating

Habits With their limited mobility mealybugs are normally found sitting, often in groups, feeding from their host plants

Breeding Females either produce fertilized eggs or live young; in some species females are parthenogenetic, with males not being known to occur

Diet Sap feeders, feeding from either the upper parts or the roots of a range of plants

Habitat Almost any kind of habitat in which their host plants grow, including houses and greenhouses; a number are pests

Distribution Worldwide, but more species in tropical regions

⊕ **Pseudococcus adonidum,** *also known as the long-tailed mealybug, is found all over the world. It is a common pest of greenhouse and conservatory plants. Length up to 0.2 inches (5 mm).*

Mealybugs

Pseudococcidae

It is a sad fact that we would rather not find many of the members of the Pseudococcidae, because most of the commonly found species are pests of cultivated plants.

THE PSEUDOCOCCIDAE ARE called mealybugs because their bodies are covered in a coating of wax particles and threads secreted by glands on the body surface, making them look floury, or "mealy." There can be so much of this wax on the outer surface that it is difficult to see the insect beneath. The wax may also extend from the rear end of the body so that the bug looks as if it has tails. While the females lack a definite head (although they do have antennae), the head of the male is quite distinctly separate from the thorax. The males lack compound eyes but do have a few single ommatidia (units from which compound eyes are built up). Both adults and nymphs suck sap from their plant hosts, often causing considerable damage. A few species of mealybugs cause the formation of galls on their food plants. Since everything they need is inside the gall, they lack legs.

Mealybug Life Cycles

The life cycle of mealybugs resembles to some extent that of the higher insects such as moths and butterflies, in which a pupal stage is present. Female mealybugs have just three nymphal instars, called crawlers, which are able to move around from one feeding point on their host plant to another. Once they become adult, the females mate (in those species that have males) or reproduce parthenogenetically. In cooler regions some species reproduce sexually, but the same species use parthenogenesis in the tropics. The males are winged and can therefore leave their food plant to find females.

Female mealybugs construct a special structure called an ovisac in which to lay their eggs. It either covers the female completely so that she can remain feeding where she is, or it

is attached to the rear end of her body. The ovisac is made from strands of sticky wax that hold the structure together. Normally between 30 and 200 eggs are laid on the food plant, but that varies according to species. Large females of *Phenacoccus aceris,* the apple mealybug, can lay thousands of eggs during their lifetime.

Male nymphs pass through just two instars. The second instar constructs a cocoon made from strands of wax in which it molts to become first a prepupa and finally a pupa. The molted skins are pushed to the outside of the cocoon by the prepupa and pupa. The final development of the nymph into the adult male takes place inside the pupa. The tiny winged males that eventually emerge may mate with one or more females in their rather short life of just a few days. The males are attracted to pheromones produced by the females.

Numerous Pests

Mealybugs are not often encountered in the wild because they are so small. There are many species, however, that are pests of cultivated plants and crops, and they are seen regularly. Some of the most damaging are the root mealybugs of the widespread genus *Rhizoecus.* All stages feed on the roots of their host plants, causing them to die back and resulting in poor growth of the plant overall. They are a great problem with cactus growers, since they can quickly destroy the plant's whole root system.

Above-ground species such as the apple mealybug have often been spread around the world as their host plant has been distributed by humans. *Phenacoccus aceris* is a real problem in North America, where it has moved from apple trees to become a pest of cherries. Not only does it cause direct damage to the cherry trees, but it also carries a virus called little cherry disease, which results in the fruits being much smaller than they should be.

⟵ *A group of European mealybugs,* Pseudococcus affinis, *feed on the stem of a passion flower vine growing in a conservatory.*

Glossary

Words in SMALL CAPITALS refer to other entries in the glossary.

Abdomen region of an ARTHROPOD's body behind the THORAX, one of three body divisions consisting of up to 10 SEGMENTS in insects

Antenna (pl. antennae) feelerlike sensory APPENDAGES mounted on the head

Appendage any limb or articulated outgrowth of the body such as ANTENNAE or wings

Arthropod a "jointed-limbed" INVERTEBRATE with a hardened CUTICLE (EXOSKELETON): includes insects, spiders, crustaceans

Biological control the use of natural predators, PARASITES, or disease organisms to reduce the numbers of a pest plant or animal

Camouflage pattern of colors designed to blend in with the background

Carnivore animal that eats meat

Chitin protein that forms an important component of many INVERTEBRATE bodies, e.g., the ARTHROPOD EXOSKELETON

Class biological grouping containing a number of related ORDERS

Compound eye the eye typical of adult insects, composed of numerous individual units (OMMATIDIA) that are marked on the surface by FACETS

Copulation the act of mating

Courtship preliminary activities that take place prior to mating and promote the coming together and correct identification of the two sexes

Cryptic coloration where the colors of an insect help it blend into its background; also referred to as CAMOUFLAGE coloration

Cuticle the external layer formed of CHITIN, which acts as an EXOSKELETON in ARTHROPODS

Diatom a single-celled alga that lives in the surface waters of seas and lakes

Exoskeleton the tough outer covering of an ARTHROPOD's body that forms its skeleton

Facet the external surface of the individual unit (OMMATIDIUM) of a COMPOUND EYE

Family a biological grouping of genera (pl. of GENUS) more closely related to one another than any other grouping of genera and always ending in -idae

Femur the third SEGMENT of an insect's leg

Gall an abnormal growth produced by a plant in response to the presence of an organism such as an insect egg. The gall increases in size as the insect LARVA inside feeds on special "grazing" tissue lining the larval chamber

Genus (pl. genera) a group of SPECIES all more closely related to one another than to any other group of SPECIES

Hemolymph the name given to the blood of insects and arachnids

Honeydew the sweet waste liquid produced by aphids and other plant bugs

Host the animal or plant with or on which another animal or plant lives and/or feeds. See PARASITE

Insemination internal fertilization of a female animal with sperm from a male

Instar the stage between molts of an ARTHROPOD. See MOLTING

Invertebrate animal lacking a backbone, as in worms, snails, insects, etc.

Larva juvenile stage between egg and adult

Mandibles the first pair of mouthparts situated on the head

Maxillae the mouthparts immediately behind the MANDIBLES

Metamorphosis process of change by which one form develops into another—usually juvenile into adult

Molting shedding of the exterior skeleton, or EXOSKELETON (verb molt)

Ocellus (pl. ocelli) simple eye of an insect consisting externally of a single FACET

Ommatidium (pl. ommatidia) the long, cylindrical single unit of a COMPOUND EYE that acts as a light receptor

Order a biological grouping of FAMILIES more closely related to one another than to any other grouping of FAMILIES

Ovipositor the structure on female insects through which eggs are laid (verb oviposit)

Parasite (parasitic) organism that lives in or on the body of another (called the HOST) and feeds on it for at least part of its life cycle

Parthenogenesis production of young by a female without having first mated with a male

Pheromone a chemical scent that produces a behavioral result in another animal, usually to attract or repel members of the opposite sex

Photosynthesis the formation of sugars and oxygen by green parts of plants when sunlight falls on them

Phylum a major group used in the classification of animals, consisting of one or more CLASSES

Polymorphism the existence, apart from the two sexes, of two or more distinctly different forms of the same SPECIES

Proboscis tubelike feeding apparatus, common in insects

Pronotum a protective shield covering the THORAX of an insect

Rostrum the piercing mouthparts of a bug; it consists of an outer sheath with inside two pairs of sharp STYLETS

Scavenger animal that feeds on dead material

Scutellum part of a bug's PRONOTUM that extends backward over the ABDOMEN; it is normally shield shaped

Segment a section of a body part, such as the ABDOMEN, ANTENNA, or leg

Species a group of organisms that in nature mate readily and produce healthy fertile offspring

Spermatophore a packet of sperm produced by male and delivered to female during courtship or mating

Spiracle an opening in the EXOSKELETON through which an insect breathes

Stridulate to generate sound by rubbing one part of the body against another (noun stridulation)

Stylets sharp mouthparts modified for piercing skin or the surface of plants

Tarsus (pl. tarsi) the series of small SEGMENTS making up the last and fifth region of the leg of insects, the end bearing a pair of claws

Thorax the region of an insect's body behind the head. It bears the legs and the wings (where present)

Tibia (pl. tibiae) the fourth SEGMENT of an insect's leg, between the FEMUR and TARSUS

Warning colors bright, distinctive colors that warn an animal's enemies that it is not good to eat and should be left alone

Further Reading

General

Arnett, R. R., Jr., and Jacques, R. L., Jr., **Guide to Insects**, Simon & Schuster, New York, NY, 1981

Barnes, R. D., **Invertebrate Zoology**, Saunders College Publishing, Philiadelphia, PA, 1987

Janzen, D. H. (ed), **Costa Rican Natural History**, University of Chicago Press, Chicago, IL, 1983

Milne, L., and Milne, M., **National Audubon Society Field Guide to North American Insects and Spiders**, Alfred A. Knopf, New York, NY, 1998

O'Toole, C. (ed), **The Encyclopedia of Insects**, Firefly Books, Toronto, Canada, 2002

Preston-Mafham, K., and Preston-Mafham, R., **The Encyclopedia of Land Invertebrate Behavior**, MIT Press, Cambridge, MA, 1993

Specific to this volume

Dolling, W. R., **The Hemiptera**, Oxford University Press, Oxford, U.K., 1991

McGavin, G. C., **Bugs of the World**, Facts On File Publications, New York, NY, 1993

Miller, S. S., True Bugs: **When Is a Bug Really a Bug?**, Franklin Watts Inc. , New York, NY, 1998

Wheeler, A. G., **Biology of the Plant Bugs**, Cornell University Press, Ithaca, NY, 2001

Useful Websites

General

http://animaldiversity.ummz.umich.edu/
University of Michigan Museum of Zoology animal diversity websites. Search for pictures and information about animals by class, family, and common name. Includes glossary

http:/members.aol.com/YEbugs/bugclub.html
Website of The Young Entomologists' Society

http://nationalzoo.si.edu/
Website of the Smithsonian National Zoological Park. Photos and information, organized by animal behavior and groups, can be found here

http://www.insectclopedia.com
Comprehensive site about the world of insects ranges from identification to bug cuisine

http://www.pbs.org/wnet/nature/alienempire/index.html
Website containing insect information

http://www.si.edu/resource/faq/nmnh/buginfo/start.htm
Encyclopedia Smithsonian entomology section (Smithsonian Museum website). Provides lively information sheets with interesting facts on invertebrates

http://www.tolweb.org/tree
The Tree of Life is a collaborative web project, produced by biologists from around the world. On more than 2,600 World Wide Web pages the Tree of Life provides information about the diversity of organisms on earth, their history, and characteristics. Each page contains information about one group of organisms

http://www.wcs.org
Website of the Wildlife Conservation Society

Specific to this volume

www.cedarcreek.umn.edu/insects/index.html
Cedar Creek Natural History Area of University of Minnesota has quite a lot of information about North American Hemiptera

http://www.earthlife.net/insects/six/html
Provides general information about Hemiptera

http://entomology.si.edu/HIS/home.lasso
International Heteropterists' Society, for serious enthusiasts

Picture Credits

Abbreviations

C Corbis; OSF Oxford Scientific Films; P Premaphotos Wildlife

t = top; **b** = bottom; **c** = center; **l** = left; **r** = right

All photographs are Ken Preston-Mafham/Premaphotos Wildlife except those listed below

Jacket
tl, tr, br Ken Preston-Mafham/Premaphotos Wildlife; **bl** John Mason/Ardea London

16–17 Dr. Rod Preston-Mafham/P; **20** Mark Preston-Mafham/P; **24** David A. Northcott/C; **24–25** Robert Pickett/C; **25** Steve Austin/Papilio/C; **26, 26–27** Science Pictures Limited/C; **27** Stephen Dalton/Natural History Photographic Agency; **34** Dr. Tony Brain/Science Photo Library; **34–35** Andrew Syred/Science Photo Library; **41** Siar Anthranir © 2000; **54, 58–59, 62** Dr. Rod Preston-Mafham/P; **76t** James Carmichael Jr./Natural History Photographic Agency; **80–81** Mark Preston-Mafham/P; **82–83** Dr. Rod Preston-Mafham/P; **87** Mark Preston-Mafham/P; **101** Science Pictures Limited/OSF; **104** Anthony Bannister/Gallo Images/C; **105** George D. Lepp/C; **106–107** OSF; **107c** Colin Milkins/OSF; **107b** Harold Taylor/OSF; **109** Pete Atkinson/Natural History Photographic Agency